Phrase-by-Phrase:

James—A Devotional Study

Rick Kavanaugh

Copyright © 2019 Rick Kavanaugh
All rights reserved
ISBN: 9781091764392

Unless otherwise indicated, all Scripture quotations are taken from the New American Standard Bible, copyright © 1960, 1962, 1963, 1968, 1971, 1973, 1975, 1977, 1995 by the Lockman Foundation.

How To Use This Study

Though this book can be used as a stand-alone study, I wrote it as a companion volume for my YouTube video study. I have created a YouTube channel titled, "Phrase-By-Phrase with Pastor Rick." I have recorded video lessons on the entire book of James. Each lesson is between two and five minutes long. They are intentionally brief to make it more convenient to have an in depth Bible study in spite of busy schedules. There are 79 lessons on James. This book is essentially the video study in written form. However, the book includes something more than the videos; questions at the end of each chapter for personal reflection or group discussion. Each chapter is intentionally brief, between one to two pages. It is different than other books in that I have not included a lot of stories and illustrations. I cut straight to the point, examining the meaning of the Biblical phrase with questions to aid in application. I would suggest watching the videos and following along in the book. The videos are free of charge. If you subscribe to my channel, then as new content is added, you will receive notifications. The address is, https://www.youtube.com/channel/UCAFNKu-Cgw Zb0cxpfnWNloQ/videos It is my prayer that you will find this study a valuable tool in your spiritual formation journey.

Table of Contents:

How To Use This Study	IV
James 1:1	1
James 1:2	6
James 1:3-4	8
James 1:5a	10
James 1:5b	13
James 1:6a	16
James 1:6b-8	18
James 1:9	20
James 1:10-12	23
James 1:13a	25
James 1:13b	27
James 1:13c	30
James 1:13d	33
James 1:14a	36
James 1:14b	38
James 1:14c	40
James 1:14d	42
James 1:14e	44
James 1:15a	46
James 1:15b	48
James 1:15c	51
James 1:16-17a	54
James 1:16-17b	56
James 1:16-17c	58
James 1:17d	61
James 1:18	63
James 1:19-20	66
James 1:21	69
James 1:22-25	71
James 1:26-27	73
James 2:1-3	76
James 2:4	78
James 2:5-7	80
James 2:8-13	83
James 2:14	85
James 2:15-17	87

James 2:18	89
James 2:19-20	91
James 2:21	93
James 2:22-26	96
James 3:1-5a	98
James 3:5b	101
James 3:6	103
James 3:6b-12	105
James 3:13a	108
James 3:13b	111
James 3:14a	113
James 3:14b	115
James 3:14c-15	117
James 3:16-17	119
James 3:18	121
James 4:1a	123
James 4:1b	125
James 4:2a	127
James 4:2b-3	128
James 4:3	130
James 4:4a	133
James 4:4b	135
James 4:4c	137
James 4:5a	139
James 4:5b	141
James 4:6-8a	143
James 4:8b-9	145
James 4:10	147
James 4:11a	149
James 4:11b-12	151
James 4:13-17	153
James 5:1-3	155
James 5:4-6	157
James 5:7-9	159
James 5:10-11	162
James 5:12a	164
James 5:12b	167
James 5:13-14a	169
James 5:14b-15a	171
James 5:15b-16a	173
James 5:16b-18	174

James 5:19-20a 177
James 5:19-20b 179
James 5:19-20c 181

James 1:1

v.1—James, a bond-servant of God and of the Lord Jesus Christ, to the twelve tribes who are dispersed abroad: Greetings.

James is a book of practical truths. It is a great reality check. Today's culture demands faith that is authentic. Unfortunately, so much of church life seems fake or disingenuous. Institutionalism has taken over the church so that much of our energy is spent trying to feed the machine. Because of that many opt out of any kind of institutional expression of spirituality. The book of James is ideally suited for this generation. James is about authenticity. The big take-a-way of this brief letter is—How do you know if your faith is authentic? How do we measure a faith that is real? If my relationship with Jesus is real, then what markers should be present in my life? Those are the kinds of questions James will attempt to answer.

James' greeting is short and to the point:

> *James, a bond-servant of God and of the Lord Jesus Christ,*
> *To the twelve tribes who are dispersed abroad: Greetings.*
> *James 1:1*

This was what is called a circular letter. That means it was passed around to various places to be read by different local church communities. Most likely people who had never met James would hear the reading of his letter. That makes his opening statement all the more interesting. He doesn't identify himself beyond his name. There were many people with that name in the ancient world, yet James only needs to state his name and people will know who he is. That is because James was the half-brother of Jesus. He is one of a very few who grew up in the same household with the King of the ages. He was the most famous person alive in the early church at that time. He didn't need to identify himself further. Talk about the opportunity to name drop! "You knew the Roman governor? That's great, but I happen to be the stepbrother of God." It would be so tempting to drop that into a conversation. But James doesn't do it. In fact, the only moniker he uses to identify himself is, *"a bond-servant of God and of the Lord Jesus Christ."*

He doesn't stress his apostleship, though he was an apostle. In fact, he was head of the Jerusalem church, but you don't hear any of that from James. He doesn't push his family connection. Instead, he identifies himself as a bondservant. A bondservant was one who voluntarily chose to remain a slave to his master for the rest of his life, even though freedom was an option.[1] Such a person had their ear pierced as a life-long declaration of their devotion.

It is also helpful to notice to whom James is writing. He addresses his message to, *"To the twelve tribes who are dispersed abroad."* These were Jewish believers who were dispersed from Jerusalem after persecution broke out. In the early years of the church, the majority of believers were Jewish. They saw the way of Jesus as the fulfillment of their Jewish religion. But those still practicing Judaism saw them as a threat. It was believed the Church was an aberration of Judaism and needed to be stamped out. Therefore, the first persecutions came from the Jews. The fledgling Christian Church was living in a hostile world and was doing all it could to survive. The faith of the early Christians was being challenged. James wrote his letter to help them understand what a genuine faith looked like. It would not look like the Judaism of their forefathers, yet they did not have to abandon their Jewish roots. However, the Church would also include Gentiles. So how could they understand this new movement? What was expected of them? What aspects of their lives would indicate their faith was real? Those are the questions James addresses in this letter.

The book seems at first glance to be a listing of random "wisdom" sayings. Some have even referred to James as the Proverbs of the New Testament. The truth is, however, James is a carefully organized letter built around ten marks of an authentic faith. My encouragement would be to read through James and focus on the ten marks.

1. Authentic Faith Is Seen in Our Response to Trials—1:2-25

James starts right out declaring that our faith will be tested. He describes the right kind of perspective to have during trial and the right kind of attitude to display. He encourages us that God will give us wisdom when facing trials, and he reassures us that trials can have a positive result if we face them the right way.

---

[1] Exodus 21:5-6

2. Authentic Faith Is Seen in a Compassionate Heart—1:26-27

Someone who has an authentic faith has a genuine care for others. But it's more than that. Most people have a sense of care for others in their lives, but for the believer, their compassion reaches out to "the other." In other words, they also care about the marginalized, the least and the neglected.

3. Authentic Faith Is Seen in Impartiality Toward Others—2:1-7

Authentic faith doesn't show favoritism for personal gain. In every culture there is always some version of a "good ol' boy's club." But that should not be found in the church. Sadly, those political viruses do infect the community of faith, but for those whose faith is genuine, favoritism is not an option.

4. Authentic Faith Is Seen in Mercy Toward Those Who Have Hurt Us—2:8-13

Those who have experienced and truly appreciated the mercy and grace that God has extended to them are inclined to extend the same to others.

5. Authentic Faith Is Seen in Good Works—2:14-26

Human works of righteousness will not save us. Salvation comes only through God's grace in response to our faith. However, if our faith is real, our life will demonstrate it through good works. Behavior does not create the reality, but rather, reality expresses itself in behavior.

6. Authentic Faith Is Seen In the Right Use of Our Tongues—3:1-12

The condition of a person's heart is seen through what they say. The tongue is an accurate thermometer of what is going on internally.

7. Authentic Faith Is Seen in Our Relationships with One Another—3:13-4:12

We can live our lives like silos, consumed with our individual responsibilities, but those who have been filled with the Spirit of God, long to participate in authentic community.

8. Authentic Faith Is Seen in Our Business Practices—4:13-5:12

When it comes to business, Christians sometimes compartmentalize their faith. What happens on Sunday and what happens on Monday are disconnected. We say, "Business is business," as an excuse for unethical or unkind practices, but that is not Biblical Christianity.

9. Authentic Faith Is Seen in Our Reaction to Sickness—5:13-18

I once had a Physician's Assistant who had a monogram stitched on his medical coat. It said, "Doctors treat. God heals." It is a beautiful symbiotic relationship. But when we are sick, is our first response to turn to God, or to seek medical attention? It's not an either/or dichotomy, but in 35 years of ministry I have seen few people who have made it a point to call for the elders to lay hands on them, anoint them with oil and pray for healing.

10. Authentic Faith Is Seen in Taking Responsibility for One Another—5:19-20

Authentic faith is more than mental ascent. Beliefs are important, but they are the beginning point of real faith, not the summation of it. James will remind us that demons have solid theology, and in fact even tremble at the presence of God, but they are irretrievably lost. A faith that is real goes beyond what we believe, and affects how we live. The implication of Scripture is that you don't really believe something until you live it.

Bethlehem was a hamlet in Israel that was so insignificant it would not even register on a map. But because of the birth of Jesus, millions of people visit there. I had the opportunity to travel to the site of Jesus' birth. I was disappointed at first to see a large church built over the location. I was expecting some kind of cave, or stable. Thankfully, churches were built over the probable sites; otherwise they would be lost to history. The thing that struck me most about visiting the birthplace of Jesus was the entrance into the church. The doorway was unusually low. People in earlier generations were on average shorter than we are to day, but that door was short even for people living a thousand years ago. I am less than average height, and yet, I had to stoop to enter the church. We learned that was intentional. The architecture was designed to proclaim that if you are going to visit the King, you have to stoop. That is the heart of James' message. He assumed the posture of a bondservant. He was willing to stoop. The question is, are we?

Reflection Questions:

1. Of the 10 areas of an authentic faith, which areas do you feel you are strong in, and where do you sense you may need some work?

2. As you read through the sections in your Bible, ask the Holy Spirit to highlight a section that will be important for you.

3. Consider making that a matter of prayer for your spiritual formation

James 1:2

v.2—Consider it all joy, my brethren, when you encounter various trials.

James begins his letter with a statement that is counterintuitive. It sounds absolutely crazy when you think about the fact that he's talking to people who are going through trials. Why would one consider something like that a joy? But this is not some naïve notion from James. He was someone who himself was martyred by the sword. So he understands that he is writing to people who are going through severe testing at that time. They're being persecuted, driven from their homes. Some are being arrested and imprisoned, and some even killed—all for being followers of Jesus. James is writing to them as one who's been in trial and one who will face the ultimate trial of martyrdom.

"Consider it all joy". Again, it sounds counterintuitive, but he's not saying to be joyful because of our pain. We don't rejoice over the fact of going through the trial. He's talking about intentionally expressing our confidence in Christ to use our trial to accomplish his purposes. That's what joy is all about. It's a deep-seated confidence that Jesus is in control and he's going to take everything that comes into our lives and use it for our benefit and ultimately for his glory. So we can rest with a calm assurance, even in the midst of trials. As a result of that assurance, we can worship God in the middle of our trials. That's what James is talking about here when he says, *"consider it all joy"*.

I'm reminded of a friend who heard those dreaded words from a doctor's lips, "You have cancer." I'll never forget when he came to me and said "Pastor Rick, I determined right there that I did not want to waste the cancer. I want to use it for Jesus' glory." Consequently, he used his journey through this trial to witness to those around him: nurses, doctors, and fellow patients he encountered, encouraging them at every opportunity. God brought a powerful miracle of healing into his life. But during that time he had no idea whether he was going to be healed or not. He used that unimaginable trial of dealing with cancer to glorify the Lord. So even in the midst of the pain of going through that trial, he was rejoicing.

Every trial is an opportunity for the life of Christ to be formed in us and for God to manifest his glory through our lives. Paul says, *"consider it all joy"* but notice he said, *"...when you in encounter various trials"*. It's *"when,"* not "if," because we're all going to encounter trials. They're going to come to us in many shapes, sizes and forms. Knowing Jesus does not guarantee that we're going to escape trials. So let's at least get the most benefit from them that we can. God may or may not cause the trial but he can use it for our good and his glory.

So here's an important caution when facing trial. I've learned that a large part of the pain is wanting to understand the "why" behind the trial. Why did this happen? Why did God allow it? Why didn't God stop it? "Why" is often the very first question we ask but it may be the last question to be answered. For some people it may not be answered until they get to heaven. There are, however, two things we can know. We can know that the trial does not have to be in vain. God can use it if we will cooperate with him. The remainder of James' opening paragraph will deal with that. We can also know that Jesus is there with us even in the midst of our trials. So when facing a trial, the question is not, "Why is this happening?" but the question should be, "How?" How can I use this to bring glory to God?

Reflection Questions:

1. In spite of the trials I am currently facing, what truths can I confidently state about God?

2. In what ways could I change my language to reflect praise when talking to others about my present trials?

3. In what ways does my relationship with Jesus supersede my present trials?

4. How can I turn my trial into a testimony?

James 1:3-4

v.3-4—knowing that the testing of your faith produces endurance. 4 And let endurance have its perfect result, so that you may be perfect and complete, lacking in nothing.

When James says that trials test our faith, he means trials exercise or refine our faith. There's nothing like trials to push our faith. They are unpleasant, but necessary because exercise produces endurance. A strong faith isn't simply a faith that can believe God for big things. Rather, strong faith is a faith that holds on.

Jesus prayed for Peter and told him that he was going to be sifted like wheat by the devil. He predicted a season when Peter would deny the Lord. He told Peter, "I have prayed for you that your faith will not fail." Peter later rejected the Lord by denying him. After Jesus' crucifixion Peter returned to Galilee to go back to fishing. But when Jesus rose from the dead, he sought Peter out in order to restore him. Peter was re-commissioned. His faith did not completely fail. It endured through trial. Peter's trial was a "sifting" that Jesus allowed because it strengthened Peter to prepare him for what he would face later. He would suffer to the point of martyrdom for the sake of seeing many souls come to faith in Jesus Christ. James is talking about a faith that holds on, a faith that endures.

Notice also the word *"produces."* James wrote, *"The testing of your faith produces endurance."* The word *"produces"* is in the present tense. That means a process is in view. James is not talking about an instant accomplishment. In fact, that is why there will be *"various trials"* involved, because the development of endurance is a process.

Endurance has a specific result. James says it this way: *"...and let endurance have its perfect result so that you may be perfect and complete, lacking in nothing." (v.4)* Notice the phrase *"so that."* That speaks to purpose. The trials produce endurance, which leads to a specific, desired result. James uses a number of descriptive terms—*"perfect, complete, lacking in nothing."* That doesn't mean we will become perfect Christians with no flaws. The *"complete"* work James is talking about is the formation of Christ in us. The Apostle Paul stated the idea in Galatians 4:19—*"My children, with whom I am again in labor until Christ is formed in you…"* The sum goal of following Jesus is, *"Christ formed"* in us.

But why is that so important that it's worth going through trials? Because the formation of Christ in us makes it possible to live out the ten marks of an authentic faith. It happens through the crucible of life, and that takes time…and it takes endurance. *"…let endurance have its perfect result."* Endurance under trial does something that nothing else can do.

Reflection Questions:

1. If you are currently facing a trial, how do you think Jesus would respond if he were in your situation?

2. In thinking about how Jesus would respond, what Christlike characteristics can you identify?

3. In addition to praying for deliverance from the trial, or strength to get through the trial, consider praying for those Christlike character traits to be formed in you.

James 1:5a

v.5a—But if any of you lacks wisdom, let him ask of God

Normally, when we come to a passage like this, we think the author is jumping to a new topic. James has been talking about trials and now suddenly, he's talking about wisdom. But notice that the sentence begins with the word *"but."* That connects us to the previous passage. This verse is talking about the need for wisdom when in the middle of a trial. When we are facing a trial, what is the one thing we really need at that moment? We may think it is deliverance, or an answer to the question, "Why?" But what we really need is wisdom. When James says, *"...if any of you lacks wisdom,"* he doesn't mean there are some people who don't need wisdom—as if they already have it. It is a figure of speech. Everyone is in need of wisdom, especially when they are in the middle of a trial.

When we are in trial, the thing we desperately need, is wisdom. But what exactly does that mean? Thomas Manton called wisdom the "skill to bear trials." I define wisdom as knowing how to live. When facing a trial, wisdom will answer some specific questions: How can I understand this trial from God's perspective? How can I navigate through this storm in such a way as to bring glory to God? How can this trial help me grow in maturity? Wisdom is not intelligence. It is not knowledge. Wisdom is about seeing life from God's perspective.

James says the way we get that wisdom is by asking—*"let him ask of God."* It is important we are clear about what James is saying. This is not about seeking answers from God. This is not asking God to tell you the next step to take, hoping he will take you by the hand and walk you along the path, step-by-step. Instead, wisdom is about seeking a new way to live. It's about looking at life from God's perspective. Rather than getting answers from God, it's about knowing the ways of God.

The primary way to gain that kind of wisdom is through the Scriptures. That is because the Bible is not an answer book; it is a wisdom book. We do not study its pages for fill-in-the-blank answers. We journey into God's word to have our minds renewed. Some people lament the fact that they can't remember the things they read from the Bible. They get frustrated because they can't retain Biblical knowledge, as if knowledge were the most important part of Bible study. Knowledge is important but it is not the most important aspect of Bible study. That may sound foreign to you, but think about it this way.

I heard this story some time ago about a grandfather who wanted to teach his grandson a lesson. So one day the grandfather took an empty, dirty basket that they typically used to haul coal. He handed the basket to his grandson and told him to take the basket down to the river, get some water and bring it back. The grandson did what his grandfather asked and went to the river and dipped the basket in river. By the time he got back to the house, of course, all the water had drained out of the basket. The grandfather sent him back again, and again the same thing happened. Each time his grandson filled the basket with water, it drained out. This happened over and over. Finally the grandfather could see his grandson was getting very frustrated. The grandfather then said, "Look at the basket and tell me what you see". The grandson said he saw an empty basket. "But what has changed?" the grandfather asked. "The basket is clean," said the little boy. As the water sifted through the basket, it washed the basket clean. His grandfather then said, "That's what the Bible does. Sometimes you study the Bible and you can't remember everything, yet it's doing a work in you, a cleansing work, a changing work in you over time."

That's what the Bible does. It renews our minds. It forms the mind of Christ in us. It helps us see life the way God sees it. We steep ourselves in the Word of God, in order to learn the ways of God.

Notice James instructs us to *"ask"* for wisdom. The word *"ask"* is in the present tense—meaning it's an ongoing process. That implies it's not an instant process—like we open up the Bible and "zap" we're blessed with the mind of Christ. Rather, it means we continually go back to the Word of God. We continually ask God to change us, to renew our mind with the mind of Christ. That way, when we are in trial, we will think the way God thinks and behave the way God behaves. When we are in trial we pray. But we don't pray "God get me out of this", or "God, speak to me from heaven and tell me why this is happening", or "God, tell me the very next thing to do." No, we say, "God, give me the mind of Christ so I can walk in wisdom and live the way Christ would live if He were living in this situation."

Reflection Questions:

1. People who see the Bible as an answer book will sometimes hunt through its pages to find that perfect verse that tells them specifically what to do in a given situation. What might be some of the problems with approaching the Bible in that way?

2. When a child is young, most parents tell their children what to do and expect the child to obey. However, if the relationship is healthy, there comes a point when the parent hopes the child will learn to make wise decisions on its own. In your relationship with your Heavenly Parent, do you behave more like the toddler who needs specific instruction, or like the maturing adult who is learning how to decide responsibly?

3. On a scale from one to ten, with one being the toddler and ten being the adult, where would you place yourself on the scale? What specific steps could you take to move yourself one or two steps closer to adulthood?

James 1:5b

v.5b—who gives to all men generously and without reproach

The word *"generously"* means giving more than we need. The book of Genesis tells the story of Joseph and his brothers. They were jealous of their brother because he was obviously their father's favorite. One day when Joseph was in the field with them, they conspired against him and sold him to some Midianites who were traveling through the area. The Midianites in turn, sold Joseph to an Egyptian official. Joseph's brothers told their father that a wild animal had killed Joseph. Jacob, the father, spent the largest part of life grieving for a dead son who, unbeknown to him, was alive. Many years later, through a series of providential events, Joseph was reunited with his brothers. When they first met, Joseph was a high official in the Egyptian government. God had promoted Joseph to a place of great power. When the brothers came before Joseph, they did not know it was him, but he recognized them. He was dressed like an Egyptian. He spoke in a different language. His brothers would have never dreamed Joseph was such a powerful man. In fact, they probably figured he had died long ago.

The story ends in a wonderful account of reunion, forgiveness and reconciliation. But at first, Joseph played some head games with his brothers. On one occasion he arranged a meal. The brothers were seated around a table, with assigned seating. He seated the brothers in order of their birth. They were stymied, wondering how he could have possibly known that. All of Joseph's brothers were half brothers, except for Benjamin. When the food was set on the table, Benjamin received five times as much food as the other brothers. It was far more food than Benjamin could have ever eaten. Joseph was saying in effect, Benjamin was highly favored and is lavished with more food than he could possibly ever eat—not because he needed it, but because Joseph wanted to honor his brother.

That is the picture of God giving generously. We don't deserve God's wisdom. Like Joseph's brothers, we have betrayed God over and over. But because we are in Christ, we are highly favored. God gives to us generously, beyond what we could ever need. God will give you more wisdom than you need. He will change the way you think.

The passage also says that God gives *"without reproach."* Maybe there is a reluctance to ask for wisdom, perhaps because we are in our trial because of our own poor choices. Maybe we have lived without wisdom and gotten ourselves into a trial. In those moments we may be tempted to think we cannot or should not ask for wisdom because, we think we are under some kind of discipline from God. No. James says to ask and God will gladly answer. He is ever gracious. If a person asks for wisdom James says, *"...it will be given to him."*

But as we saw in a previous study, we must continually ask. We must earnestly seek God's wisdom. The writer of Proverbs expressed the intensity of the pursuit:

> *20 Wisdom shouts in the street, She lifts her voice in the square; 21 At the head of the noisy streets she cries out; At the entrance of the gates in the city she utters her sayings: 22 "How long, O naive ones, will you love being simple-minded? And scoffers delight themselves in scoffing And fools hate knowledge? 23 "Turn to my reproof, Behold, I will pour out my spirit on you; I will make my words known to you... 3 For if you cry for discernment, Lift your voice for understanding; 4 If you seek her as silver and search for her as for hidden treasures; 5 Then you will discern the fear of the Lord and discover the knowledge of God. 6 For the Lord gives wisdom; From His mouth come knowledge and understanding. Prov. 1:20-23; 2:3-6*

When you go through trial, what are you looking for; deliverance, escape, reasons why, next step instructions? Or, are you looking for wisdom—the mind of Christ, to live like Christ in order to glorify Christ?

Reflection Questions:

1. When you have prayed in the past concerning a trial, was wisdom your first concern, or were you more interested in deliverance?

2. It is only natural to want out of the pain. In what ways would our priorities need to change if we were to be more interested in wisdom than deliverance?

3. Can you think of one or two areas in your life where you might need to make a priority adjustment?

4. What could be one practical step you could take to demonstrate you are changing your priorities?

James 1:6a

v.6a—but he must ask in faith without any doubting

In our previous study, verse 5 said that God gives wisdom to us when we ask, and he gives generously without reproach. But there is a condition. We *"must ask in faith without doubting"*. God will give wisdom to those who are in trial, who are seeking the mind of Christ in order to understand how to behave in a Christ-like way when in a trial. But this person has to ask in faith and without doubting.

The word for *"doubting"* in Greek is *diakrino*. It means to "judge between the two" or "to distinguish between the two". The picture that comes to mind when I think of this word is someone walking down a trail and they come to a fork in the road. They can't decide which way to go—they start down the left, but then second-guess themselves. Then they turn back to the right. They vacillate back and forth. That's the meaning of this word. The question might be, "What two options is the person choosing between?"

We ask for wisdom, which means we are asking for the mind of Christ. Where exactly is the fork in the road? Remember, we are not talking about God giving us specific answers. We are not looking for that specific verse that tells us to do XYZ on a specific date. We are asking for wisdom. When we ask for wisdom, we're asking for our minds to be renewed. We are asking that God would reshape our thinking so that we see our situation from God's perspective. We are asking for the mind of Christ.

The wisdom of Christ is immensely helpful when facing trial, but it also affects the rest of our lives. That's really where the rub comes in. We start down the right side of the fork toward the wisdom of Christ to face our trial, but then when that same wisdom calls us to apply the mind of Christ in the other areas of our life, there is a danger we might balk. Do we really want the mind of Christ in every area of our life?

Paul describes what it looks like to live with the mind of Christ in Philippians 2:3-8:

> *Do nothing from selfishness or empty conceit, but with humility of mind, regard one another as more important than yourselves. Do not merely look for your own personal interests, but also for the interests of others. Have this attitude in yourselves which was also in Christ Jesus, who, although he existed in the form of God, did not regard equality with God a thing to be grasped, but emptied himself, taking on the form of a bondservant and being made in the likeness of men. Being found in appearance as a man, he humbled himself by becoming obedient to the point of death, even death on the cross.*

Jesus considered the needs of others to be more important than his own needs. He lowered himself in order to lift others up. That's the mind of Christ. So when we're praying for wisdom and asking God to help us view the world through his eyes—to see it the way he sees it, to think the way he thinks—that's the mindset that Jesus had. We are not just asking for wisdom to know what to do in a trial. In reality, we are asking for a total makeover in the way we think, the way we behave. That's the small print behind this great promise. The person who doubts is the person who vacillates because they want wisdom for the trial but they're not sure they want the mind of Christ for the other parts of their life.

When we pray for wisdom to walk through trial in a way that glorifies God, we have to take on the mind of Christ. To do that means we have to empty ourselves and put others first. That's what we're really praying for when we pray for wisdom. James says if we're double-minded and vacillate between these two ways of life, then we will not receive God's wisdom. It's all or nothing. You're either all in or you're out.

Reflection Questions:

1. When thinking about your own faith formation journey, would you see yourself as one who is all in, or would you honestly admit you are hesitant about giving every part of your life completely to Christ?

2. If you are hesitant to go "all in," can you identify any reasons for the hesitancy?

3. In what ways could you pray specifically to overcome those points of hesitancy?

James 1:6b-8

v.6b—for the one who doubts is like the surf of the sea, driven and tossed by the wind. For that man ought not to expect that he will receive anything from the Lord, being a double-minded man, unstable in all his ways.

We want wisdom, but when we realize it's a total make over, we pause. But that puts the brakes on God's plan, which is to form Christ in us. It's all or nothing with Jesus. He said that if we were going to be his disciples we had to take up our cross daily and follow him. You carried a cross for only one purpose—to die. We are called to take "self" to the place of execution every day. There are some who want the mind of Christ, but they don't want that. James comments on that kind of individual, *"That man ought not to expect that he will receive anything from the Lord."* (v. 7) Jesus doesn't expect us to be perfect, but he does want us to be "all in."

That's the challenge, but here's an encouragement: doubt is not an emotion that comes on us that we have no control over. Rather, it is a choice of the will to both seek and obey God or to do our own thing. We can choose to follow Jesus. James goes on to describe the doubter as, *"...a double-minded man, unstable in all his ways."* (v.8) The Greek word for double-minded literally means, "two-souled." This is a person with a split allegiance. They want to think the way God thinks, but they don't want to love the way God loves. But James is encouraging us to be different than that. When facing trial, we pray, "God change my mind to the mind of Christ, because I am all in and I am trusting that this trial will be used by you to conform me to the image of Christ."

The final goal when it comes to trials is stated in Romans 8:28-29:

> *28 And we know that God causes all things to work together for good to those who love God, to those who are called according to His purpose. 29 For those whom He foreknew, He also predestined to become conformed to the image of His Son*

It doesn't say that God is going to cause everything to be good, because sometimes trials don't turn out well. Just look at Hebrews chapter 11 where we see all the great men of faith who suffered severely, being sawn in two, sewn up in animal skins, thrown to the wild beast, burned alive, hanged, tortured—it did not turn out *"good"* for them. What Paul actually says is that *"we know that God causes all things to work together for good."* All things may not turn out *"good,"* but God uses the trial to bring about goodness.

That promise, however, is specifically for those who *"love God and are called according to his purpose."* That's the key. We have to be called according to God's purpose. So what is the purpose? He tells us in verse 29, *"...for those whom he foreknew, he also predestined to become conformed to the image of his son."* That's what the *"good"* is—conformity to the image of his son. We love God and we're called to his purpose, which is to be conformed to the image of Christ. God takes all of our trials and he works those together for that end purpose, to conform us to the image of Christ. That's what trials are all about.

Reflection Questions:

1. If you are going through a trial presently, what are some ways you can use your trial to bring glory to God?

2. In what ways would a person's approach to Scripture change if they were in the word to gain wisdom, instead of simply seeking answers?

3. The mind of Christ considers the needs of others to be more important than their own needs. If that were to be true in your own relationships, how would your behavior change toward others?

James 1:9

v.9—But the brother of humble circumstances is to glory in his high position

Though this verse may seem like a new topic, James is still speaking in the context of trials. One of the greatest trials we face is financial. That was especially true in James' day. Many of the Christians he wrote had been driven from their homes and were being heavily persecuted. A good deal of the persecution was financial. Their homes were confiscated and their assets were seized. They were literally stripped of everything they had.

In that culture there was a strong belief that when God favored someone, he blessed him or her financially. People assumed that if someone were suffering physically or financially, then God's curse was upon them.

The disciples believed that way. When Jesus and his disciples encountered a man who was born blind, they asked Jesus, "Lord, who sinned, this man or his parents that he was born blind?" It was the natural assumption that if somebody was suffering, he or she must have done something wrong. However, Jesus corrected their thinking and said it was neither; it wasn't him or his parents. He said, "This man is going to bring glory to the name of God."

James is addressing a people who have been struggling financially, even though they trusted in Christ. Their wealth was being stripped away. Their livelihood was adversely affected to such an extent that they were having trouble surviving. They must have wondered, "Is this God's curse? Are we doing the wrong thing? Is God judging us?" James wanted to help them by giving them the right perspective. So in verse 9 he wrote, *"...but the brother of humble circumstances is to glory in his high position."*

The phrase *"brother of humble circumstances"* is referring to the poor. James is saying that this person needs to see himself or herself as being in a high position...as being rich. In fact, the word *"glory"* means, "to celebrate his true condition," "to celebrate where you are." Here's the Bible's assessment of true wealth: *"Blessed be the God and father of our Lord Jesus Christ who has blessed us with every spiritual blessing in the heavenly places in Christ Jesus." (Ephesians 1:3)*

God has blessed us with every blessing, but it says every *"spiritual"* blessing. Then Paul describes those blessings as he talks about eternal life. We are adopted into God's family, we have redemption, we are free from sin and guilt, we have forgiveness, we're given the gift of innocence and we are given the knowledge of God's plan for the ages. We also received the Holy Spirit as a down payment for the future inheritance we are going have in full. Those are all the riches that God gives to those who love him. (See Ephesians 1) Therefore, even those who are financially poor are rich beyond imagination.

Someone might say that sounds good in theory but what good does it do to tell the poor person whose children are barefoot that he needs to glory in his spiritual riches in Christ? What good are spiritual riches to a man like that?

All I can do is recount to you a situation that helped me better understand this spiritual concept. I had an opportunity to travel to India and spend time with some of the poorest people in the world. Yet those people were so full of praise, gratitude and generosity, that I've never seen anything like it. I remember the family we stayed with insisted we stay in their home, while they slept in a shack with a dirt floor. I felt guilty doing that, but they wouldn't consider anything less than giving us their best.

We were there to teach pastors by holding seminars. They would travel for miles and miles, some even in bare feet, to come to where we were teaching. I recall it was cold there at that time of the year. One of the young men in particular took a liking to me and, for whatever reason; he wanted to give me his shawl or coat. I didn't want to take it. I already had 10 coats at home. I didn't need it and he did because it was cold. But he wanted me to have it and I was told that I would offend him if I didn't take it. So I took it. And when I did, I could see the joy in his face when he gave it to me. Here was this man who had literally nothing in this world, yet he gave me the coat off his back. He was so thrilled and filled with joy to be able to do that that I felt like I was in the presence of people who were truly Christ-like. Was I there to teach them? I felt like they were teaching me so much as I watched how they lived. They literally had nothing but they were so generous and giving. As I watched their lives, I thought to myself "that is true wealth." Those were people who understood what they have in Christ and they were celebrating at a level that I can't even begin to comprehend.

Reflection Questions

1. Is it wrong for the poor to seek to better their financial condition?

2. If not, are there any conditions or parameters that would apply?

3. When do we cross the line between having riches and trusting in them?

James 1:10-12

vs.10-12—and the rich man is to glory in his humiliation, because like flowering grass he will pass away. For the sun rises with a scorching wind and withers the grass; and its flower falls off and the beauty of its appearance is destroyed; so too the rich man in the midst of his pursuits will fade away. Blessed is a man who perseveres under trial; for once he has been approved, he will receive the crown of life which the Lord has promised to those who love Him.

Earlier James talked about the poor man glorying in his high position. Now he talks about the rich man glorying in his humiliation. There is a debate among scholars as to whether this rich man that James is referring to is a Christian or not. If he is a Christian, then perhaps James is alluding to the fact that this rich person may be stripped of his riches because Christians were under great persecution during this time. If he's speaking to a non-Christian, then perhaps he is warning this person of their destiny, the density that all of us will face...death. Ultimately, they need to be aware of what true riches are.

Either way, James is drawing a distinction, but he's' calling both the poor and the rich to a true view of wealth. The admonition is to glory in his humiliation; in other words to see life from its true perspective. Here's the reality of life in James 1:10, *"...like flowering grass he will pass away."* The stark reality is, that no matter what station we are at in life, it will be over soon.

Then James says, *"For the sun rises with a scorching wind and withers the grass; and its flower falls off and the beauty of its appearance is destroyed; so too the rich man in the midst of his pursuits will fade away."* Right in the midst of life, before the wealthy person even realizes it, life is gone. James stresses the rich here because they're the ones who are going to be tempted to depend on their wealth.

Money is a great tool but money is neutral. Money isn't going to help us in the day of death. James is warning people to get their priorities straight now, because life will be over before they know it. In the final analysis, both the rich and the poor who persevere under trial should look forward to the crown of life that God has promised to those who love him.

That's what James 1:12 says, *"Blessed is the man who perseveres under trial; for once he has been approved, he will receive the crown of life which the Lord has promised to those who love him."* This whole section in James is dealing with trials as it relates to finances and how we respond to those trials.

Reflection Questions:

1. If someone were to take an objective look at the way you manage your finances, would they view you as a steward or would they view you as a consumer?

2. Is there anything in your answer that might nudge you to adjust your approach to your personal finances?

3. What one small adjustment could you make that would move you closer to the position of a steward?

James 1:13a

v.13a—Let no one say when he is tempted, "I am being tempted by God"; for God cannot be tempted by evil, and He Himself does not tempt anyone.

This verse is still connected to the subject of trials. The Greek word for trial and for temptation are the same word. God allows trials into our lives, but with those trials can come temptation. For example, there may be a spouse who is going through the trial of a negligent partner. That's the trial, but the temptation might be to cheat on that spouse. The neglected partner may be tempted to find affection in the arms of another person. God can take the trial of the person who is in the difficult relationship and use it. But God does not cause the temptation that sometimes accompanies the trial. Yet sometimes people blame God for the temptation.

James makes two very strong statements in verse 13. First, he says God cannot be tempted by evil. Then he says that God himself does not tempt anyone. Those are important ideas and we need to take time to examine each of them. I'm going to take several posts to try to unpack these ideas.

The first one says God cannot be tempted by evil. So right out of the gate there seems to be a problem. If God cannot be tempted then how do we explain that Jesus was tempted by the devil in the wilderness? That was the very beginning of his ministry. How could he be tempted if he's God yet God cannot be tempted? We can either say that Jesus is not really God or we can say that Jesus was not really tempted. Those statements contradict Scripture and neither answer is satisfactory. So we need to figure this out. This is more than just academic interest to us. The temptation of Jesus provides our hope of an empathizing God, one who understands what we go through. It helps us relate to a God who can feel our pain and can empathize with us when we are tempted. It's important to us that we have a God who is an advocate for us because he understands us.

There are some foundational truths we need to establish right at the beginning when we start unpacking all of this. One of those is that Scripture clearly teaches Jesus is God. In Colossians 2:9 where it's talking about Jesus it says, *"...in him all the fullness of deity dwells in bodily form."* So it's very clear that he, Jesus, is God.

Also, Scripture teaches that it is impossible for God to sin. 1 John 1:5 says, *"this is the message that we have heard from him and announced to you that God is light and in him there is no darkness at all."* There is no moral impurity or sin in God. Therefore, it is impossible for Jesus to sin because Jesus is God. So how do we explain him being tempted if he can't sin? How could his temptation be real if he can't sin? Those are some things we will begin to look at next time.

Reflection Questions:

1. Can you think of a trial you have experienced where you were specifically tempted to sin?

2. When the temptation came, can you recall the frame of mind you were in or the attitudes you had during the trial?

3. Identifying those things might help you uncover some triggers to which you may be susceptible. Can you identify what those may be?

James 1:13b

v.13b—Let no one say when he is tempted, "I am being tempted by God"; for God cannot be tempted by evil, and He Himself does not tempt anyone.

In the last study we talked about Jesus being God and how God cannot be tempted, yet Jesus was tempted. How do we reconcile those ideas? There are realities that will help us make sense of this apparent dilemma.

Jesus is one person with two natures. Theologians would say he is inseparably united, but not commingled or commixed. Let me paint a word picture that might help that make more sense. Salt and pepper are two distinct items. You can mix them together, but they still retain their differences. The salt does not become the pepper and the pepper does not become the salt, though mixed together. That is different than, for example, mixing two colors of paint. If you mix blue paint and yellow paint, you get green paint. There are no longer two distinct colors of paint, but instead, a third color. You can't separate the green paint to once again make blue and yellow. Yet you can separate the salt and the pepper to make two distinct items. Jesus is like the salt and pepper, not like the blue and yellow paint. He is one person (the Son of God) with two distinct natures (human and divine). His two natures are inseparable, but distinct. He is not a third new being, but one person with two natures. He will forever be the God-man.

Getting ahold of that helps us understand the apparent contradictions between his two natures. For example, as God, Jesus is omnipotent (all powerful). Yet after preaching all day, he was so tired he fell asleep in the bow of a boat and slept through a storm—that is, until his disciples woke him in fear for their lives. Then he stood and spoke to the storm and instantly the winds stopped blowing and the sea was completely calm.

Jesus is omniscient (all knowing). As God he knows all things and can read people's minds. And yet, he does not know the time of his second coming to earth. He said only the Father has that knowledge. (Mark 13:32)

Charles Hodge, an 18th century theologian and professor at Princeton Theological Seminary wrote:

> As a man is one person and all his acts are the acts of that one person, so all the acts of Christ are the acts of His whole person. Some are purely divine, like creation and preservation; some are purely human, like eating, drinking, and sleeping; some are acts in which both natures concur, like the work of redemption. Yet all these acts are the acts of Christ, of one and the same person. It was Christ who created the world. It was Christ who ate and drank. And it is Christ who redeems us from the power of darkness.[2]

Because the two natures are distinct, it is possible for Jesus to be tempted in his human nature, but it is not possible for Jesus to be tempted in his divine nature. But even there the temptation is different than man's temptation. The source of Jesus' temptations and the source of our temptations are different. Temptation's source with fallen man comes from our fallen nature. *"But each one is tempted when he is carried away and enticed by his own lust. Then when lust has conceived, it gives birth to sin; and when sin is accomplished, it brings forth death." (James 1:14-15)*

It is impossible for God to be tempted in that sense, since he has no sinful nature to entice him to do evil. So the temptation did not originate from within him, but was external to him and came from Satan. In the sense of an inner, carnal enticement, we can say it is impossible for God to be tempted. Jesus has no carnal lust from within to attract him to sin. Any external appeal that Satan could direct toward Jesus could only be directed toward Jesus' humanity, for Satan's authority only extends to the earthly realm. Satan has no authority over God.

Because of that, even though Jesus was tempted, it was not possible for him to sin. I know there are many who would disagree with me on that point. That's fine. Let's agree to disagree. Some think the fact that Jesus could not sin, weakens his temptation. But it actually makes it worse, which we will see next time.

Reflection Questions:

---

[2] Paul Kjoss Helseth, "Charles Hodge on the Doctrine of the 'Adorable Trinity'", Southern Baptist Journal of Theology 21.2, 2017, Accessed February 2019, http://equip.sbts.edu/wp-content/uploads/2017/09/SBJT-21.2-Hodge-on-the-Trinity-Helseth.pdf

1. Does the idea that Jesus could be tempted in his human nature, but not in his divine nature, encourage you in your own battle against temptation, or discourage you? Why?

2. Some would say that if Jesus could not be tempted in his divine nature, than his empathy toward us in our struggle is not real. What do you think about that?

James 1:13c

v.13c—Let no one say when he is tempted, "I am being tempted by God"; for God cannot be tempted by evil, and He Himself does not tempt anyone.

I left off in the last study by saying that the fact that Jesus could not sin does not diminish the force of his temptation. In fact, it actually increases it. Some struggle with this because they feel his temptations were not legitimate if he could not have sinned. They believe his empathy is somehow hollow unless he could sin. "How can his temptation be real?" they ask.

Even though he could not sin, he still felt the weight of the temptation, and he felt it at a level we could never comprehend. Have you ever gathered wood for a fireplace? I remember holding out my arms like a forklift while a partner piled the chunks of wood onto my arms. We often tried to see who could hold the most sticks of wood. There came a point where I could not hold anymore. If my partner had placed another piece of wood on me, I would have dropped the entire pile. We have a limit to what we can carry. Temptation is the same way. The enemy places temptation after temptation on us until eventually we collapse. We all have a threshold to what we can handle, and we all have given in at some point. There is not one of us who hasn't crossed the line from temptation to sin. Except for Jesus. Satan threw everything he had at Jesus. He never let up, never relented, but Jesus stood firm. We would have collapsed long before, but Jesus endured it. He understands the weight of our temptation, because he endured every bit of it, and then more because he never gave in to the attacks. There have been times when you were tempted, and you felt the weight of the temptation, but you resisted. Right? That's how it was with Jesus, except he never gave in one time. So he knows what it is to be tempted far beyond anything we could ever comprehend.

Therefore, when we look at Matthew's story of Jesus being tempted, and compare it to James' statement that God cannot be tempted, we come to two conclusions.

1. Jesus can totally empathize with our struggles because He has felt the full force of Satan's attacks.

What does this mean? To empathize means to listen, but it is a certain kind of listening. It is a kind of listening that is not defensive, nor critical, nor suspicious. It is the opposite of the kind of listening that a jury does when listening to witnesses. It is sympathetic listening; believing the story of the other. Empathy also means participating in the other person's story, so that the listener actually feels the experience at some level. The empathizer enters into the experience of the other. That's what Jesus does. He hears your heart's cry and feels your struggle. He gives a sympathetic ear. He listens as a friend who wants to help.

> *15 For we do not have a high priest who cannot sympathize with our weaknesses, but One who has been tempted in all things as we are, yet without sin. 16 Therefore let us draw near with confidence to the throne of grace, so that we may receive mercy and find grace to help in time of need. — Hebrews 4:15-16*

2. Jesus is not in the least threatened by the work of Satan.

Do not think this battle in the wilderness was a conflict between equals. Satan was no match for Jesus. The devil may have thought he was seeking to un-throne the king, but that is not what was actually taking place. The Bible says the Holy Spirit drove Jesus into the desert to be tempted by the devil. That's because the wilderness temptation was actually Jesus laying down the gauntlet. It was Jesus' declaration of war on Satan. He faced all the enemy had and beat him. He was saying, "I am serving notice that your time is up. You are defeated."

Jesus did not face Satan's temptations to give us an example to follow. He wasn't modeling for us how we should fight the devil. He was demonstrating that there is only one who has ever fought the devil and won. He doesn't want us to try and imitate him and go head to head with Satan. Instead, he wants to live in us and have us allow him to fight the enemy through us. Jesus was in effect saying, "I am the only one who has ever beat him, so let me do it for you." The entire temptation episode means Jesus understands your problems and he is big enough to handle them.

Reflection Questions:

1. When you are tempted, do you envision it as you facing the enemy by yourself, or do you see it as you and Jesus facing the enemy together?

2. I suspect for most people, they think of it as facing the enemy alone. If you were to change your perspective, in what ways would you react differently when facing temptation?

3. Can you think of two or three things you might do next time you are tempted that would reflect an understanding that you are fighting this battle with Jesus, rather than facing it alone?

James 1:13d

v. 13d—Let no one say when he is tempted, "I am being tempted by God"; for God cannot be tempted by evil, and He Himself does not tempt anyone.

James says in this verse that God *"does not tempt anyone."* But we see places in Scripture where the very opposite seems true; take 1 Kings 22, for example. In this passage Ahab, king of Israel, requested assistance from Jehoshaphat, king of Judah, to go to war with Syria. Jehoshaphat agreed, but wanted to ask the Lord for direction. Ahab summoned his prophets and they assured Jehoshaphat of victory. Evidently Jehoshaphat wasn't comfortable with this advice, so he asked if there were any more prophets in the land. Ahab reluctantly admitted there was Micaiah, but Ahab hated him. He was a true prophet of the Lord and told the truth. Jehoshaphat insisted, so Ahab brought him to court. As Ahab feared, Micaiah predicted defeat. Jehoshaphat and Ahab still went to war. They were defeated and Ahab was killed. The prophet's words, as recorded in 1 Kings, implicate God in a deception:

> *19 Micaiah said, "Therefore, hear the word of the LORD. I saw the LORD sitting on His throne, and all the host of heaven standing by Him on His right and on His left. 20 The LORD said, 'Who will entice Ahab to go up and fall at Ramoth-gilead?' And one said this while another said that. 21 Then a spirit came forward and stood before the LORD and said, 'I will entice him.' 22 The LORD said to him, 'How?' And he said, 'I will go out and be a deceiving spirit in the mouth of all his prophets.' Then He said, 'You are to entice him and also prevail. Go and do so.' 23 Now therefore, behold, the LORD has put a deceiving spirit in the mouth of all these your prophets; and the LORD has proclaimed disaster against you."—1Kings 22:19-23*

In this passage we have God putting a lying spirit in the mouth of the prophets. Yet we read passages like our text that says God cannot tempt, along with other statements that say God cannot lie (Titus 1:2; Hebrews 6:18). How do we answer this discrepancy?

In the case of 1 Kings, we are bumping up against an example of progressive revelation. In the beginning of Israel's history, God offered limited information about himself, and over time expanded man's knowledge of him. For example we read in Genesis that the redeemer will come through the human race (Genesis 3:15). We learn later that the redeemer will come specifically from the family of Abraham (Genesis 12). It isn't until many generations later that we learn he will sit on the throne of David (1 Samuel) and that he will be born in Bethlehem (Micah 5).

Not only was information about God limited, but so also was information about the devil. In 2 Samuel 24 we read the story where David was tempted to number Israel. He did so against God's will and then God disciplined him. The thing that is odd about that story is that it says God is the one who moved David to count the people. But then God turned around and punished him for it. We read this same story again in 1 Chronicles 21, only in that account it is the devil who tempted David to number Israel. 1 Chronicles was written a couple hundred years after 2 Samuel. In the early years the Israelites attributed everything to God—good and evil. But over time their concept of a Satan grew, so that by the time 2 Chronicles was written they understood it was not God who tempted David, but Satan. That's how progressive revelation works, and that's what we see going on in the story with Ahab and Jehoshaphat.

Furthermore, the passage in Kings was a vision; so we don't know if it really happened. But even if it did, it was a Jewish idiom to says God caused the spirit to go. In all likelihood, it was in the deceiving spirit's mind to deceive Ahab, and God permitted it as the means to bring about the judgment Ahab deserved. Progressive revelation makes it clear that God doesn't tempt anyone.

Reflection Questions:

1. Blaming God for our sin has been a part of our nature from the beginning. Adam blamed Eve and Eve blamed the serpent. Think back to a time when you gave in to temptation. Can you recall excuses you made?

2. When we sin, there is a tendency to justify our behavior—perhaps not to completely excuse, but at least to soften the indictment against us. What do you think God is looking for in our confession and repentance?

3. What attitude adjustments or behavioral changes do you need to make in your confession practices?

James 1:14a

v.14a—But each one is tempted

God does not tempt, so where does temptation come from? Some would say it comes from the devil. That is true in some instances, but James reveals a more common source. In fact, in the next section he teaches us several important points about temptation.

The first thing I noticed in this verse was the universal nature of temptation. *"But each one is tempted."* By saying that each one is tempted, James is saying that everyone is tempted. Temptation is the universal experience of mankind. Paul wrote, *"No temptation has overtaken you but such as is common to man." (1 Corinthians 10:13)* I like the way it is stated in the New Living Translation. *"But remember that the temptations that come into your life are no different from what others experience."*

This point hardly needs to be supported. We know temptation is universal for Romans 3:23 says, *"All have sinned and fallen short of the glory of God."* James' point is that because literally everyone is tempted, we can conclude that there is no temptation that is unique. Some people may see that fact as an excuse to sin. In other words, they may reason that temptation is part of human nature so we can't be blamed for our sin. It is a natural part of who and what we are.

One woman wrote just such a sentiment on her blog:

> I'm human. I am admittedly full of lustful thoughts. I can't help it. God made me a catty creature. I have indulged in certain extra-curricular activities and enjoyed them immensely. People can deny their corrupt human nature all they want. But it's there inside all of us. So, I've decided that I'm going to embrace my human nature for what it is.

This woman's reasoning is not an isolated exception. I believe she represents the general thinking of the population. If sin is universal, it must be natural. If everybody's doing it, then it must be okay. Yes, temptation and sin are universal. Yes, temptation and sin are natural. Left to our selves that's exactly where we will end up, but it's not okay.

We would never do that in the physical realm. If we allow things to take it's natural course in the physical realm, then we would not seek to immunize people from disease. But we do treat disease in an attempt to stop the natural course of things, and eradicate the disease. Sin is a spiritual disease. Left to itself, it will spread like a cancer and destroy the soul. That may be natural, but it's not normal.

So we cannot use the universality of sin and temptation as an excuse to succumb to it. James' point is that the universal nature of temptation forces us to the opposite conclusion. Because temptation is universal we cannot use the excuse that our temptation is unique, that our situation is different and thus we should be excused from our temptation. So we can't say, "Everyone's doing it so I can." Nor can we say, "My situation is unique." We are all tempted, so how do we beat it? That's what James will unfold in the phrases that follow.

Reflection Questions:

1. What are the most common sources of temptation in your life?

2. What are some reasons that you find it hard to avoid them?

3. What are some choices you could make to reduce the amount of temptation in your life?

4. Would such changes be important enough to alter your behaviors / habits? Why/ Why not?

James 1:14b

v.14b—But each one is tempted

Notice the last two words of that phrase—*"is tempted."* It's in the present tense, which means it never stops. We're not just tempted once in a while, but we are tempted continually. There is no safe place from which to escape temptation.

We are bombarded with images from the moment we awake until we lay our head down at night. The forbidden fruit is dangled before us in every imaginable way; from TV adds to magazine covers, from Internet advertisements to radio broadcasts, from the common culture of seductive dress to the allure of riches and wealth. Temptation is everywhere.

We could blame our decadent culture for the continual barrage of temptation, except that temptation is just as common in other parts of the world where it's not shamelessly displayed for all to see. We constantly face temptation, and it always follows the same pattern.

> *15 Do not love the world nor the things in the world. If anyone loves the world, the love of the Father is not in him. 16 For all that is in the world, the lust of the flesh and the lust of the eyes and the boastful pride of life, is not from the Father, but is from the world.—1John 2:15-16*

John speaks in this passage about *"the lust of flesh."* That speaks of hedonism, which says the pursuit of pleasure is the highest good. The *"lust of the eyes"* refers to materialism, which says that matter is the only reality, so get all you can. The *"boastful pride of life"* speaks of humanism, which says that man's answers to life rest within himself.

These tactics were used with Eve in the very beginning. The serpent tempted Eve to eat from the tree of the knowledge of good and evil. The fruit was desirous to eat, which is the lust of the flesh—hedonism. It looked good to the eyes, the lust of the eyes—materialism. And it promised fulfillment. Eve believed if she ate the fruit she would ascend to her deserved station in life and be as God—*"the boastful pride of life,"* humanism.

Satan used these same temptations on Jesus. He tempted Jesus to turn stones into bread, after Jesus had been fasting for forty days. That was the hedonistic lust of the flesh. He used the lust of the eyes when he showed Jesus all the kingdoms of the world in an instant of time and offered them to Jesus if he would bow down to Satan. That was the lust of the eyes—materialism. He tempted Jesus to step off the pinnacle of the Temple. He quoted Scripture that said the angels would catch him. It was a known custom that the Messiah would make a grand entry into the world and what better way to do that than to drop over fifteen stories and be caught by angels. Surely that would make it clear to the people who Jesus was. That was the boastful pride of life—humanism.

He repeats the same patters with us. Those patterns come at us over and over. We never get beyond the point of temptation. Because of that, we must be on the alert, and not let our guard down. We can't take a vacation from vigilance, because it is at those moments when we want to relax that we're most likely to be tempted. That seems discouraging, but there is hope, as we will see. But first we need to understand the nature of temptation more fully, which we will see in the other phrases of this verse.

Reflection Questions:

1. Thinking about the times you are most often tempted, would you identify your most common temptations as the lust of the flesh, the lust of the eyes, or the boastful pride of life?

2. Thinking in those categories, what are some triggers that pull you into a battle with temptation?

3. What alternative activities can you think of that could help you avoid those situations?

James 1:14c

v.14c—when he is carried away and enticed

So far we've looked at the universal nature of temptation, and the continual nature of temptation. Next, James identifies the tactical nature of temptation. James says a person is *"carried away and enticed."* That phrase describes how temptation actually works. The phrase *"carried away"* means "to draw out." The tempted individual is drawn out from some place. The natural question would be, drawn out from where? What does that mean?

It seems to indicate being drawn out from a place of safety, because the next word, *"enticed"* conveys the picture of catching something with bait. Evidently, before we are drawn out we can't be effectively enticed. There's something about leaving where we are, and being removed to a different place where we are unprotected that makes us vulnerable to the bait.

The battlefield of the spirit is always fought in the mind. I would submit to you that the tactic that's used is to draw the mind away, to pull our focus off of the things of God so that we will be easily enticed.

Scripture emphasizes the need to keep our minds focused in the right place:

> *Finally, brethren, whatever is true, whatever is honorable, whatever is right, whatever is pure, whatever is lovely, whatever is of good repute, if there is any excellence and if anything worthy of praise, dwell on these things.—Philippians 4:8*

> *Your word I have treasured in my heart, that I may not sin against You.—Psalms 119:11*

Satan drew Eve away from the safety of God's Word by speaking error to her. He confused her by asking, *"Indeed, has God said, 'You shall not eat from any tree of the garden'?" (Genesis 3:1)* Then later, he directly contradicted God. *"The serpent said to the woman, 'You surely will not die!'" (Genesis 3:4)*

He got her to focus on that one tree of prohibition, instead of all the trees of Gods' permission. Once her mind was pulled away from God's Word, he enticed her. It was then that she looked at the fruit and saw that is was desirous. The battlefield is in the mind. That is why we have to be careful about unguarded input. We will see and hear many harmful or inappropriate things in the course of a day. In many regards, such things are unavoidable. The issue, however, isn't trying to eliminate that kind of stimulus; like a monk who hides away in the desert. But we do need to be perceptive about what we are hearing and seeing. We must recognize input for what it is and even pray about it in the moment. Notice when bait is being set. Pay attention to possible traps.

Reflection Questions:

1. What are the sources in your life that are the most hazardous temptation traps?

2. Give an example of a simple prayer you could pray in those moments when you recognize a trap is being set?

3. When heading into situations you recognize are common trigger points for you, what are some things you could do to prepare yourself in case a trap is set?

James 1:14d

v.14d—by his own lust

This phrase reveals the conspiratorial nature of temptation. It's not our environment that leads us to sin. It's not even the devil; though both of them are factors. The place to set the blame is our own lust. Adam blamed his environment. He pointed to Eve as a poor influence. *"The man said, 'The woman whom you gave to be with me, she gave me from the tree, and I ate.'" (Genesis 3:12)* Eve blamed the devil. *"And the woman said, 'The serpent deceived me, and I ate.'" (Genesis 3:13)* Even though both pointed the finger to someone else, they were each held accountable for their own actions.

Our environments, other people and even the devil are factors in our temptations, but the real enemy is our own lust. The problem is not the tempter without. It's the traitor within. We must be aware of this so we take responsibility for our own actions instead of blaming the devil or other people. This also means the enemy is around us as long as we are there.

The Apostle Paul wrote, *"For I know that nothing good dwells in me, that is, in my flesh; for the willing is present in me, but the doing of the good is not." (Romans 7:18)* This is not a positive view of human nature, but Paul understood that once someone sins, a spiritual disease begins to spread inside him or her. I describe that nature as a lust orientation. We often think of lust in relation to sex, but it's much bigger than that. Lust is an inward focus, where everything must be what I want, when I want it, the way I want it. All arrows are turned inward, so that it is all about me. It's like an emotional black hole that pulls everything in on itself. It is the opposite of love, which has an "others focus."

We think the opposite of love is hate, but it's not. The opposite of love is lust. We are either self-focused, or others-focused. That orientation can set us up for temptation. I doubt, however that any of us are all one way or the other. We are probably on a sliding scale, and the dial moves back and fourth. At times, we operate closer to the love end of the scale, and at other times, closer to the lust end of the scale.

Reflection Questions:

1. In which environments do you tend to tip the scale toward lust: work, family, marriage, friends, church, self?

2. What things could you do or say in those environments that might help you stay focused on others, instead of self?

James 1:14e

v.14e—by his own lust

The phrase, *"his own"* reveals the individual nature of temptation. Temptation is customized. I remember looking out the window of my host home one morning while on a short-term mission trip to Swaziland, Africa. Beyond the edge of the yard was a large mound of trash. A dog was rummaging through it. I could tell the dog was totally into whatever it was gnawing on. It looked like garbage to me, but to the dog, it was a feast. There was nothing in me that would attract me to that garbage, but to the dog it held great appeal. There was something in the dog that was attracted to the trash. What attracts humans and what attracts dogs is different. But also, what attracts one human and what attracts another human is different.

Temptation is tailor fit to your personal preferences. Each person's soul has its own patterns of fleshly desire as a result of his or her environment, upbringing, and personal choices. Each person has their own triggers that catch them up. This is why we should not sit in judgment of others who sin. The things that trapped them may not tempt us, but we must not judge the splinter in their eye when we have our own logs to worry about.

Paul wrote, *"Brethren, even if anyone is caught in any trespass, you who are spiritual, restore such a one in a spirit of gentleness; each one looking to yourself, so that you too will not be tempted." (Galatians 6:1)* That doesn't mean we will be tempted with the same sin as the person who was caught in a trespass, but our condemning pride can blind us to our own weaknesses, which leaves us unguarded and vulnerable.

It is important to understand our individual attractions and weaknesses so that we can be prepared to flee what we may recognize as a possibility for temptation. But also, we must be careful not to judge others who are around things that would attract them, but not us.

Reflection Questions:

1. Can you be brutally honest and admit to a time when you looked on someone else who was caught in a sin with contempt or judgment?

2. What was so different between their sin and yours?

3. It has been said that when we examine someone else's sin, we judge their actions, but when we look at our own sin, we judge our motives. Has that been true of you? If so, what steps could you take to change that tendency?

James 1:15a

v.15a—Then when lust has conceived, it gives birth to sin

This phrase reveals the conditional nature of temptation. Temptation alone is not sin. There is a condition that must occur before sin is committed. Sin only results when lust is conceived. The question is, what constitutes conception? Certainly it is acting upon the temptation, but Jesus took it further into the realm of motive and thought.

> *21 You have heard that the ancients were told, 'YOU SHALL NOT COMMIT MURDER' and 'Whoever commits murder shall be liable to the court.' 22 "But I say to you that everyone who is angry with his brother shall be guilty before the court; and whoever says to his brother, 'You good-for-nothing,' shall be guilty before the supreme court; and whoever says, 'You fool,' shall be guilty enough to go into the fiery hell—Matthew 5:21-22*

> *27 You have heard that it was said, 'YOU SHALL NOT COMMIT ADULTERY'; 28 but I say to you that everyone who looks at a woman with lust for her has already committed adultery with her in his heart—Matthew 5:27-28*

For sin to be conceived, there must be an internal agreement with the temptation that precedes the act. The inner acquiescence is tantamount to committing the deed, but until there has been an inner reception to the temptation, sin has not occurred. That is why temptation is an internal battle. The mind, will and emotion are attacked in temptation.

Let's say a person's life is represented by a three-legged stool. Those legs represent the three places temptation attacks. All three legs must be knocked out from under a person before she or he falls into sin. The first leg represents the mind, the second represents the emotions and the third represents the will.

1. The First Leg—The first wave of attack is waged against the mind. The plan of attack is two-fold: First, the aim is to get us to doubt God's word. Second, the aim is to get us to believe we can gain some type of personal

advantage outside of God. That's what the serpent did with Eve. He sowed doubt by asking, "Did God really say you couldn't eat from that tree?"—as if to suggest she was mistaken. Then he talked about how God was holding out on her and that if she partook of the tree she would reach her fullest potential—but she had to do that without God.

2. The Second Leg—The second assault comes from the world and is targeted at the emotions. The tool here is enticement. The things of the world are placed in our path to lure us into the trap.

3. The Third Leg—The third assault targets the will. When we fall to temptation it often seems as if someone else is running our lives. We can't believe we "did it". Have you experienced those moments when on the other side of the temptation you could clearly see how stupid you were, but when in the midst of the situation it was as if your mind shut down? If you have, then you are not alone. It is a common experience. We will look more closely at that later.

There is good news and bad news in this. The good news is, only we alone can knock out this leg of our table. The enemy can't force our will. The bad news is, once the other two legs are knocked out from under us, it's almost impossible to resist the temptation. The will is designed to lead our lives, but it is wired to do so by the council of our minds. When the mind is deceived the will is left to receive input from the emotions, but our emotions are not trustworthy. They need the discipline and restraint of the mind. Without that, the emotions are pulled toward the flesh and become an undue influence upon the will. That is when we cave into the temptation.

Reflection Questions:

1. Have you had an experience where temptation hit and it seemed as if your mind turned off? Can you describe what that was like?

2. When facing temptation, where do you think the battle should be fought: at the place of the mind, the will or the emotion? Why?

3. Which of the three do you think is your weakest link?

4. Can you think of any action steps to strengthen that part of your life?

James 1:15b

v.15b—when sin is accomplished, it brings forth death.

Here we have the consequential nature of temptation. Sin always leads to death. For the unsaved this is ultimately hell. But James is writing to believers. He's saying that for the Christian, there is a death that takes place when sin is committed. Death means a severing from our environment. In the way a letter is "severed" from the environment of an envelope, the spirit is severed from the body at death. When a marriage dies the two partners are severed from each other. Death is always about separating something from its environment. For the Christian, there is a severing that takes place when they sin.

The culprit that leads us to sin is our own lust. When we sin, we are separated from the influence (read environment) of the Spirit.

> *For the flesh sets its desire against the Spirit, and the Spirit against the flesh; for these are in opposition to one another, so that you may not do the things that you please. (Galatians 5:17)*

There's a severing—a joining ourselves to the nature of lust within—and a separating of self from the influence of the Spirit. That leads to destruction; a form of death. Paul wrote, "*...for if you are living according to the flesh, you must die." (Romans 8:13)* The reason sin leads to destruction in the believer is because we become like the one we obey. (Romans 6:16) We become conformed to our lust instead of the image of Christ. That's dangerous because lust is a monster that can never be satisfied. Frederick Buechner wrote in *Wishful Thinking: A Theological ABC*, "Lust is the craving for salt by a man who is dying of thirst."[3]

An anonymous author who told his story years ago in *Leadership Magazine* revealed the destructive nature of lust.

---

[3] Buechner Frederick, *Wishful Thinking: A Theological ABC,* New York: Harper & Row, 1973.

> I learned quickly that lust points in only one direction. You cannot go back to a lower level and stay satisfied. Always you want more. A magazine excites, a movie thrills, a live show really makes the blood run. I never got as far as outright prostitution, but I've experienced enough of the unquenchable nature of sex to frighten me for good. Lust does not satisfy; it stirs up. I no longer wonder how deviants can get into child molesting, masochism, and other abnormalities. Although such acts are incomprehensible to me, I remember well that where I ended up was also incomprehensible to me when I started.[4]

Lust keeps driving us toward a place where we are dead to life. We can't enjoy true pleasure without perverting it. We are never satisfied. And we forfeit the purpose for which we were truly created.

Ronald Meredith, in his book, *Hurryin' Big for Little Reasons*, describes one quiet night in early spring:

> Suddenly out of the night came the sound of wild geese flying. I ran to the house and breathlessly announced the excitement I felt. What is to compare with wild geese across the moon? It might have ended there except for the sight of our tame mallards on the pond. They heard the wild call they had once known. The honking out of the night sent little arrows of prompting deep into their wild yesterdays. Their wings fluttered a feeble response. The urge to fly—to take their place in the sky for which God made them-- was sounding in their feathered breasts, but they never rose from the water. The matter had been settled long ago. The corn of the barnyard was too tempting! Now their desire to fly only made them uncomfortable. Temptation is always enjoyed at the price of losing the capacity for flight.[5]

---

[4] This story was taken from an article of Leadership Journal, a pastor's magazine from Christianity Today. I read the article over 15 years ago and cannot locate it. But I have included the link to the magazine. https://www.christianitytoday.com/pastors/leadership-journal-archives/

[5] Meredith Ronald, *Hurryin' Big for Little Reasons,* Nashville, TN: Abgindon Press, 1964.

This is perhaps the worse consequence, that Temptation is always enjoyed at the price of losing the capacity for flight. A person loses the ability to be intimate with God because spiritual intimacy is founded on love, which requires selfless giving: while lust produces a selfish hoarding that pulls everything in on itself like a black hole. In that state there can be no intimacy. We have lost the capacity for flight. So how do we beat temptation? That's what we will look at next.

Reflection Questions:

1. When we think of the destructive nature of sin, we often relate it to the big things: adultery, murder, theft, etc. In what ways is sin destructive, even in the "little" things?

2. Why do you think sin is sinful—is it just because God gave a command and we broke it, or do you think something more is involved? If so, explain what you mean.

3. If we are aware of a sister or brother who has stumbled into the destructive pattern of sin, what kinds of things should we as a loving friend do to help them?

James 1:15c

vs.14-15—But each one is tempted when he is carried away and enticed by his own lust. Then when lust has conceived, it gives birth to sin; and when sin is accomplished, it brings forth death.

So far we have looked at the universal nature of temptation, the continual nature of temptation, the tactical nature of temptation, the conspiratorial nature of temptation, the individual nature of temptation, the conditional nature of temptation, and the consequential nature of temptation. Now the question is, how to beat temptation?

Temptation is a battle, so we need to be ready to fight. Keeping that in mind, I will share a few ideas using battle language. There are five things we can do to stand firm against temptation.

1. Gather Useful intelligence—Successful armies do reconnaissance to gather important information. For us, that's implanting the Word of God. Without the Word dwelling richly within us, we are unable to stand when the time of testing comes. When you read the temptation narrative of Jesus, you will notice that he answered Satan with Scripture. He had committed the Scriptures to memory.

2. Stay out of hostile territory—Whenever possible, flee the temptation, and do it the moment the temptation comes. Don't stand there and debate the issue. Get out of wherever you are. A literal change of scenery can make a great difference. That's because temptation introduces anxiety, and that triggers the reptilian brain. The high learning center of the brain is called the neocortex. That's the part of the brain we use for reasoning and language. The reptilian brain is the instinctual part of our brain. It runs the involuntary functions of the body, like blood pressure, temperature, heartbeat, etc. This is the last part of the brain to die. When someone is technically alive—meaning they are breathing and the heart is beating—but they are unconscious and unreceptive to stimuli, it's the reptilian brain that is functioning.

The reptilian brain also operates the flight or fight reaction. When anxiety is introduced, the blood rushes to our extremities, preparing us to either flee or fight. It's instinctive. When that happens, the blood flow to the neocortex is restricted, so our reasoning powers are diminished. In a sense, our brains shut off. We aren't thinking in our right mind. When temptation comes, it triggers the reptilian brain, so that our reasoning powers are diminished. Research shows that if a person will take fifteen minutes to refocus (a brisk walk, reading something out loud, etc.) blood flow will return to the neocortex and reasoning powers will be restored.

3. Engage early warning systems—Know your triggers and be on the alert. What are the conditions that most often lead you to defeat? Learn what triggers your reactions. A prayer that might be helpful is King David's prayer: *"Search me, O God, and know my heart; try me and know my anxious thoughts; and see if there be any hurtful way in me, and lead me in the everlasting way." (Psalm 139:23-24)* Once we are aware of our triggers, avoid them—or at least be wary of when they are tripped. The great reformer, Martin Luther, once said, "Don't sit near the fire if your head is made of butter."[6]

4. Sound the Alarm—Cry out of the Lord as soon as temptation strikes. If you wait too long, you won't call for deliverance. Then it will be too late.

5. Expend your ordinance—Use the Word of God as a weapon. You cannot argue against the enemy. You must fight with God's Word. When I am attacked, I speak out loud to the enemy. I do not believe he can read our minds. So, like Jesus in the wilderness, I talk out loud. One tool you can use is to write a key passage of Scripture on a card, or type it in your phone. When you are aware of a temptation, speak out loud and in the name of Jesus command the enemy to leave. Then read out loud the Scripture you recorded. For example, if fear is a trigger and you sense anxiety coming on, you might say something like the following:

> Enemy of God, in the Name of Jesus Christ I command you to leave me alone for the Word of God says, "The Lord is my light; whom shall I fear? The Lord is the strength of my life; of whom shall I be afraid?"

Reflection Questions:

---

[6] Maher, Raymond, "Don't Sit Near the Fire if Your Head is Made of Butter", News-Optimist, March 2017, Accessed February 2019, https://www.newsoptimist.ca/opinion/columnists/don-t-sit-near-the-fire-if-your-head-is-made-of-butter-1.11047512

1. Which of these techniques would be most difficult for you to use, and why?

2. Which of these techniques do you think would be most helpful for your present situation, and why?

3. What Scripture can you think of that would best address your most persistent temptation?

James 1:16-17a

vs. 16-17a—Do not be deceived, my beloved brethren. Every good thing given and every perfect gift is from above,

Trials come into our lives and we can get discouraged if we look at things from a wrong perspective. We can get derailed because we don't understand why God has allowed the trial. And then with the trial often comes temptation, and we can incorrectly think God has caused the temptation since He allowed the trial. James has told us that God doesn't tempt us. Temptation comes from our own lust. But he also wants us to understand that when God does allow trials in our lives they are allowed for good reason. God doesn't randomly allow trials. There's always a purpose.

Notice James begins this section by warning them about deception—*"Do not be deceived."* He's concerned his readers will be deceived at this point. When our world is turned up side down we can think all kinds of incorrect thoughts about God. James wants to make sure we understand where God is when life is falling apart, because to be deceived—to think incorrectly about God—will only add misery to your situation.

First James warns them to not be deceived because a good God only gives good gifts. *"Every good thing given and every perfect gift is from above, coming down from the Father of lights." (v.17)* God blesses us with many things. He abundantly supplies our needs. He fills our lives with many expressions of his kindness. If you were to read verse 17 in isolation, that's how you might interpret it. We might see it as a promise that God gives us all kinds of wonderful things to enjoy. Certainly we are grateful for those times when He does do that, but in order to properly interpret this verse we have to read it in context. The overall theme since the beginning of this letter has been trials and tribulations. That understanding needs to shape our view of this verse.

James uses the term *every* two times—*"every good thing,"* and *"every perfect gift."* This certainly includes the rich blessings we enjoy, but *every* also includes the gifts God brings into our lives that we may not enjoy. In other words, Scripture characterizes the trials that God allows into our lives, as God's gifts to us. That may sound strange, but it will make sense if we understand two things, which we will look at in our next study…

Reflection Questions:

1. In what ways might you be able to characterize your trials as God's gifts?

2. Thinking back over past trials, identify something good that came out of them.

3. Do you think it was an example of God causing the trial to bring about that result, or was it more a matter of God taking a trial and causing something good to come from it?

James 1:16-17b

vs.16-17b—Do not be deceived, my beloved brethren. Every good thing given and every perfect gift is from above

Last time we saw Scripture characterizes the trials that God allows into our lives as God's gifts to us. That sounds strange, but will make sense if we understand two things. First, we need to know why God gives us the gifts he does. James indicates there are two reasons for these particular kinds of "gifts." God gives us what is for our good. The text mentions, *"Every good thing given." "Good"* means good in the sense of what is best for us. It does not mean that which brings joy or pleasure, but that which is for our benefit; like surgery. We need it, but there is no pleasure in it.

What is *"good"* is determined by God's grander purposes, not our personal comfort. When God promises good things for your life, what you think that means and what he means may be different. And if we are not clear on that point, then we can end up disappointed with God, because we think he didn't come through for us. When, in fact, the problem isn't that he didn't keep his promise, but that we simply had the wrong expectation. Take the subject of healing, for example. John Piper writes,

> Christ's healings are a sign of the in-breaking of the Kingdom of God and its final victory over all disease and all the works of Satan. It is right and good to pray for healing. Christ has purchased it in the death of his Son, with all the other blessings of grace, for all his children. But he has not promised that we get the whole inheritance in this life. And he decides how much. We pray and we trust his answer. If you ask your Father for bread, he will not give you a stone. If you ask him for a fish, he will not give you a serpent. It may not be bread. And it may not be a fish. But it will be good for you. That is what he promises.[7]

---

[7] Piper, John, "Ten Aspects of God's Sovereignty over Suffering and Satan's Hand in it", Desiring God, Desiring God 2005 National Conference, October 2005, Accessed February 2019, https://www.desiringgod.org/messages/ten-aspects-of-gods-sovereignty-over-suffering-and-satans-hand-in-it.

The second thing we need to know is that God gives us the "gifts" he does for our completion. James speaks of *"every perfect gift."* The word *"perfect"* refers to completeness or being of full age. This is something that God gives us that has an intended purpose, and God is committed to see that purpose through. The Apostle Paul wrote, *"For I am confident of this very thing, that He who began a good work in you will perfect it until the day of Christ Jesus." (Philippians 1:6)* God allows trials into our lives and though they are difficult, when they have completed their total work the results will be a gift from God. We see this idea in places like Romans 5:3-4:

> *And not only this, but we also exult in our tribulations, knowing that tribulation brings about perseverance; and perseverance, proven character; and proven character, hope*

Reflection Questions:

1. Identify any ways you have grown as a result of past trials.

2. What was it about the trial that allowed you to grow?

3. Is the trial the "gift", or is the opportunity associated with the trial the "gift?"

4. In what ways could you pray to thank God for his "gifts"?

James 1:16-17c

vs.16-17c—Do not be deceived, my beloved brethren. Every good thing given and every perfect gift is from above, coming down from the Father of lights,

So far we have seen that God allows into our lives that which ultimately will be for our good--"*every good gift*"—and he allows that which works toward our completion—"*every perfect gift*". But not only do we need to know why God gives us the "gifts" he does, but also, we need to know the kind of God who gives us these "gifts." James describes God in three ways in this section. These descriptions are important because they will reassure us we can trust God when his "gifts" don't make sense.

1. We Trust God because He Operates from an Elevated Perspective

v.17—Every good thing given and every perfect gift is from above, coming down. This is a way of expressing the exalted position of God. He sees things from a different perspective. One of the most disillusioned groups in the world would have been Jesus' disciples. They had hoped that Jesus would restore Israel to national glory, that he would break the yoke of Roman oppression. But instead of defeating the Romans, Jesus was killed by them. All their hopes were pinned on him and he let them down. If a man who can walk on water, raise the dead and cast out demons cannot defeat the Romans, then no one can. What they didn't understand—what they couldn't understand—was that Jesus' death was the intended way to victory. They did not realize that Jesus came to defeat something much greater than Rome. He came to destroy death and sin. The only way to do that was to absorb the disease of sin into himself and then destroy it by dying on the cross. In being condemned, he condemned sin and death. But the disciples couldn't see that. Even Lucifer himself didn't understand it. Paul wrote in Corinthians that if he had, he would not have influenced the rulers to destroy Jesus. (1 Corinthians 2:8)

Jesus walked two of his disciples through the entire Old Testament to show them it had predicted his necessary death. Until Jesus pointed it out, they missed it. He saw it because he was looking with a divine perspective. In fact, when he first told Peter he would die, Peter tried to dissuade him. But Jesus rebuked him. He said, *"Get behind me Satan. For you are thinking like man and not like God." (Matthew 16:23)* Peter was looking at things from an earthbound perspective. That is what happens when we enter trial. We see it from our limited perspective, unable to understand it from God's point of view. He knows what he is doing, even though he doesn't tell us.

2. We Trust God because He Operates with Exalted Power

God is called *"the Father of lights"* in this passage. James uses the definite article, which means we should read that phrase as follows: *"**THE** Father of lights."* This is speaking of God as the creator of the heavens. The Psalmist captured it well.

> *To Him who made the great lights,*
> *For His lovingkindness is everlasting:*
> *The sun to rule by day,*
> *For His lovingkindness is everlasting,*
> *The moon and stars to rule by night,*
> *For His lovingkindness is everlasting. (Psalms 136:7-9)*

As the Father of lights, He is sovereign. How does that affect us? Paul answered that. *"And we know that God causes all things to work together for good to those who love God, to those who are called according to His purpose." (Romans 8:28)*

We need to be clear about what this verse does and does not say. This does not say that everything will turn out the way we hope. This does not say that our painful situations will have a happy ending. This does not say this is a promise for everyone. This does, however, say God providentially orchestrates life's circumstances to bring good out of them. But the good is identified by the passage: *"For those whom He foreknew, He also predestined to become conformed to the image of His Son, so that He would be the firstborn among many brethren" (Romans 8:29)* God will cause everything to work together for the purpose of conforming us to the image of His Son. But that promise is limited. It is only to those who love God and are called according to his purpose. And that purpose is conformity to his Son.

The "gifts" that come into our lives are like ingredients in a cake. Taken separately, some are wonderful and some are nasty. A spoonful of brown sugar…yum! But have you ever had a spoonful of vanilla? It smells great, but by itself, it is terribly bitter. But when all the ingredients are mixed together to produce a cake—it's culinary magic. A. J. Conyers in *The Eclipse of Heaven* said, "The extreme greatness of Christianity lies in the fact that it does not seek a supernatural remedy for suffering, but a supernatural use for it."[8]

Reflection Questions:

1. If Jesus were going through the same trial(s) you were going through right now, in what ways do you think he might react?

2. What "Christlike" qualities would he exhibit?

3. In what ways can God use your trial(s) to produce those same qualities in you?

4. How might that change the way you pray during your trial(s)?

---

[8] A. J. Conyers, *The Eclipse of Heaven: The Loss of Transcendence and It's Effect on Modern Life*, South Bend, IN: St. Augustines Press, 1999.

James 1:17d

v.17—with whom there is no variation or shifting shadow

So far we have seen that we can trust God because he operates with an elevated perspective and with exalted power. This next phrase tells us he can be trusted because of his unchangeable character. James says that with God there is *"no variation or shifting shadow."* He is describing what theologians call immutability. That means that God cannot change. For example, God cannot learn. If he could, it would indicate there is knowledge he does not yet possess. But God is omniscient, or all knowing. Malachi 3:6 says, *"For I, the LORD, do not change."* And Hebrews 13:8 says, *"Jesus Christ is the same yesterday and today and forever."*

But some may wonder, doesn't the Bible say that God changed his mind? What about the story of Noah's flood? Didn't the Bible say that God was sorry he made man? That's because God's character never changes, but his dealings with people does according to their interaction with him. For example, God told Nineveh he was going to destroy them in 40 days because of their sinful way. However, when Jonah preached a message of impending judgment, they repented, so God relented. When Scripture says God never changes, it is referring to his nature, his character and his purposes.

That's incredibly important when we think about our trials. Because when life crashes down around us we wonder where God is. We ask, "How could he do this? Can I trust him to keep his word?" The Bible, however, teaches that God is love. That's the center of his character. No matter what you are going through his love has not altered one bit. Paul reassured us on that point with these words:

> *Who will separate us from the love of Christ? Will tribulation, or distress, or persecution, or famine, or nakedness, or peril, or sword? Just as it is written, FOR YOUR SAKE WE ARE BEING PUT TO DEATH ALL DAY LONG; WE WERE CONSIDERED AS SHEEP TO BE SLAUGHTERED. But in all these things we overwhelmingly conquer through Him who loved us. For I am convinced that neither death, nor life, nor angels, nor*

principalities, nor things present, nor things to come, nor powers, nor height, nor depth, nor any other created thing, will be able to separate us from the love of God, which is in Christ Jesus our Lord. (Romans 8:35-39)

Reflection Questions:

1. Some people believe that to say God operates from an elevated perspective—that he knows and sees things we cannot know—and thus, we cannot always understand what he is doing…some say that kind of an answer is a copout. How do you reconcile the difficult things in life with a God who seems absent or impotent?

2. God doesn't take time to explain himself. Even the first sentence of Genesis doesn't defend the existence of God. It just states that God is. Why do you think God doesn't explain himself?

3. Do you find it difficult to worship a God you cannot understand, or does the mystery of how God operates enhance your awe of Him? Why or why not?

James 1:18

v.18—In the exercise of His will He brought us forth by the word of truth, so that we would be a kind of first fruits among His creatures.

This verse describes the big picture of what God is doing in our lives. Let's unpack this a phrase at a time.

"He brought us forth." This speaks of the ultimate gift from God. The literal translation of the phrase is "to bring forth from the womb, to give birth to." That is speaking of our spiritual birth, which is the ultimate gift from above.

"In the exercise of his will." It was God's will to bring us forth. God initiated our spiritual birth. Salvation is rooted in God's will, not our goodness. John said it as clear as anyone. *"But as many as received Him, to them He gave the right to become children of God, even to those who believe in His name, who were born, not of blood nor of the will of the flesh nor of the will of man, but of God." (John 1:12-13)*

"By the word of truth." Our spiritual birth happened via the proclamation of the good news, God's truth. God's ultimate gift came to us by means of the gospel. *"So faith comes from hearing, and hearing by the word of Christ." (Romans 10:17)*

"So that we would be a kind of first fruits among his creatures." This is the goal of God's salvation gift. *"First fruits"* refers to the choicest item, or to the beginning of something. Jesus is referred to as the first fruits of the resurrection, signifying that there will be others who will resurrect as well. When James speaks of his readers being *"a kind of first fruits among his creatures,"* he could be referring specifically to his immediate audience since they would be the first converts. But in a broader sense, it speaks of man's unique position in creation. We are the choicest of creation because more than any other creature, we are trophies of God's grace.

God selected you to show how awesome He is; that He could take a sinful, selfish creature and transform him or her into a child of God. Heaven will stand amazed at his workmanship. This is what God is hoping to achieve in us. But someone may ask, "Isn't allowing us to suffer so he can be glorified cruel and egotistical?" No, because people find their greatest happiness in God's greatest glory. Our greatest happiness will be in magnifying God's glory because that is the end to which we were created. Charles Spurgeon said it well.

> God's great design in all His works is the manifestation of His own glory. Any aim less than this is unworthy of Himself. But how shall the glory of God be manifested to such fallen creatures as we are? Man's eye is not single, he has ever a side glance towards his own honor, has too high an estimate of his own powers, and so is not qualified to behold the glory of the Lord. It is clear then, that self must stand out of the way, that there may be room for God to be exalted; and this is the reason why He often brings His people into difficulties, that being made conscious of their own folly and weakness, they may be fitted to behold the majesty of God when He comes forth to work their deliverance.[9]

> *Beloved, do not be surprised at the fiery ordeal among you, which comes upon you for your testing, as though some strange thing were happening to you; but to the degree that you share the sufferings of Christ, keep on rejoicing, so that also at the revelation of His glory you may rejoice with exultation. If you are reviled for the name of Christ, you are blessed, because the Spirit of glory and of God rests on you. 1 Peter 4:12-15*

Reflection Questions:

1. Suffering and trials are unpleasant and any normal person does not want to experience them. So how might your trials result in God's glory?

2. How is it possible that someone's suffering could bring glory to God?

3. Paul wrote, *"That I may know Him and the power of His resurrection and the fellowship of His sufferings, being conformed to His death." (Philippians 3:10)* Why would someone want to have a fellowship in

---

[9] Charles Spurgeon, *Morning and Evening*, Grand Rapids, MI: Discovery House, 2016.

Christ's sufferings, to be conformed to his death? Is that even healthy? What is Paul getting at?

4. When you look at Paul's request compared to your own, what implications does that have for your own spiritual growth?

James 1:19-20

vs. 19-20—This you know, my beloved brethren. But everyone must be quick to hear, slow to speak and slow to anger; for the anger of man does not achieve the righteousness of God.

At this point, there is a shift in James' instruction. He has been speaking of deception, warning his people not to be deceived. But now he acknowledges that they have understanding. *"This you know, my beloved brethren."* The problem James is addressing here is not so much deception concerning trials, as it is inappropriate reaction to trials. In spite of our knowledge about trials we can still be defeated in the midst of them. It's true; we must not be deceived concerning them. We must have the right knowledge, but also, we must respond strategically. *"This you know, my beloved brethren. But everyone must be quick to hear, slow to speak and slow to anger; for the anger of man does not achieve the righteousness of God."* (James 1:19-20)

The wrong response when trials come is to be *"quick to speak."* Generally this comes out as complaint or fear. That often leads to anger. We become angry at God for allowing the trial, or at people who caused the trial, or at life in general, simply because we hate being in trial. But when we respond in anger, it sabotages the purpose of God. He can use the trial for our good, but if we respond in anger it can short circuit what God is trying to do. *"For the anger of man does not achieve the righteousness of God."*

Anger stops the work God is doing in us through the trial. This is because what we know can be overcome by our emotions and our emotions can be fed by our words. We can literally talk ourselves into a state. Have you ever done that? You start complaining to yourself and you get worked up until you are madder than a hornet. And no one's even around. It's just you and the trees.

The right response when in trial is to *"Be quick to listen."* James is referring to listening to the Word of God, which is the subject of his next paragraph. Notice the word *"quick."* When difficulty hits, run quickly to God's Word so it will shape your thinking. John Piper writes:

Christ's priorities of what he wants for you is so different than your priorities, that if you don't begin to get your mind saturated with Jesus' way of thinking, then you won't be able to make sense out of the pain in your life. You will tend to get angrier and angrier - because your priorities are, "if he loved me then.....", and you provide a list of all your demands and its not his list, it's not the way Jesus thinks, because what he values are hearts that are so enamored with him that they shine more clearly when everything we were leaning on is gone."[10]

In the very middle of a trial, when I am feeling fear and sorrow and pain, if I am asked by a friend, "How can I pray for you?" I might ask them to pray for the disease to be healed, or for my financial needs to be met, or for the people to stop doing the things that are hurting me.

It would be natural to think of the pain and how to stop it, but instead, our chief concern should be that we stay faithful so that we will glorify God in the way we endure what he has deemed best.

One anonymous author put it this way:

> I asked for strength that I might achieve;
> I was given weakness that I might obey.
>
> I asked for health that I might do great things;
> I was given infirmity that I might do better things.
>
> I asked for riches that I might be happy;
> I was given poverty that I might be wise.
>
> I asked for power that I might have the praise of men;
> I was given weakness that I might feel the need of God.
>
> I asked for all things that I might enjoy life;
> I was given life that I might enjoy all things.
>
> I received nothing I asked for,
> But everything I hoped for.

---

[10] John Piper, "Job", Suffering.net, n.d. Accessed February 2019, http://www.suffering.net/piper1.htm.

Let us live as Jesus prayed, *"My Father, if it is possible, let this cup pass from Me; yet not as I will, but as You will." (Matthew 26:39)*

Reflection Questions:

1. Sometimes when we get in a situation we start complaining to our selves before we realize what we are doing. On a scale of one to ten (1 = never, and 10 = always) where would you place yourself when answering the question—Do I complain when facing a difficult situation?

2. What are the reasons you think people tend to default to complaining rather than defaulting to prayer when facing difficulties?

3. What does the tendency to complain, rather than pray, say about our faith?

James 1:21

v. 21—Therefore, putting aside all filthiness and all that remains of wickedness, in humility receive the word implanted, which is able to save your souls.

The paragraph begins with the word "*therefore.*" This sentence is both a conclusion and a launch point. It is a conclusion in this sense; James has instructed us to run to the Word when in trial, instead of being *"quick to speak and quick to anger."* That's because the anger of man does not achieve the righteousness of God, which is the goal of the permitted trial. But how do you run to the Word? What does that mean exactly? This passage is a launch point in that it answers those questions and moves away from the topic of trials and begins to focus on the Word of God.

James answers that by instructing us, "*putting aside all filthiness and all that remains of wickedness."* This is the first thing that has to be done if a believer is going to benefit from the Word. There has to be a commitment to lay moral depravity aside. This is not about perfection, but it is about intent. Notice the word *"putting."* It's in the present tense, both in English and in Greek. It refers to an ongoing process. That infers that putting aside filthiness and wickedness is a constant battle. Notice also James speaks of *"all that remains of wickedness."* As a believer, wickedness has been put out of our lives, but there are still traces. We live in the world and its filth contaminates us. We have to regularly seek to keep ourselves pure. Think of Peter when Jesus washed the disciple's feet in the upper room. Peter didn't want Jesus to do it. It was too much of a role reversal. Peter should be washing Jesus' feet, not the other way around. But Jesus told Peter if he didn't allow Jesus to wash his feet then Jesus would have nothing to do with Peter. In typical fashion, Peter went to the other extreme and told Jesus to give him an entire bath. Jesus responded by saying he didn't need a bath. They were already clean. (He was speaking metaphorically; because he made a side reference that one of them wasn't clean, referring to Judas). Jesus told Peter that all he needed was a foot washing. That is us—we don't need a bath. That salvation cleansing has already taken place, but we do need to clean the contamination of the world off us. And that is a constant battle.

James goes on to tell us that in addition to the commitment to stay clean, we need to turn to the Scriptures. *"In humility receive the word."* Humility is living in proper dependence on God. The opposite of that would be independent pride that seeks to handle everything in one's own strength. Approaching the Word with humility means we must depend on the Holy Spirit to illuminate our minds and hearts when reading the Scriptures. That also means approaching the Word with a teachable and pliable spirit. We come to the Scriptures with no agendas. We don't superimpose our own ideas upon the text. But we allow it to speak to us.

In addition to that, James reveals how the Bible works. He speaks of *"the word implanted."* When we hear God's Word, it is implanted, like a seed. It's that seed that changes us. In other words, when we hide a passage in our heart it works on us. The initial reception of the Word is only the beginning of its work. Once received it will grow and produce results beyond the initial effect. The work it accomplishes is expressed by the phrase, *"which is able to save your souls."*

The word *"save"* means to heal. God's word produces healing in us. The body, mind and spirit are healed through the Word of God. The Bible is more than ink on a page. It is the doorway to divine encounter.

Reflection Questions:

1. What remnants of *"wickedness"* or *"filthiness"* threaten to contaminate your life?

2. Some exposure to the evils of the world are unavoidable. However, there may be steps we can take to lessen the world's grip on us. Can you think of any changes you could make to mitigate worldly contamination?

3. Do you set aside time to meditate on the Scripture? Do you spend time thinking deeply about a passage or verse? Is that a practice you would be willing to take up? Why or why not?

James 1:22-25

v.22—But prove yourselves doers of the word, and not merely hearers who delude themselves.

A hearer who deludes himself or herself is someone who thinks that acknowledgement and agreement with the Word is the same as obeying the Word. To grasp, acknowledge and even agree with a truth does not mean the truth is applied to one's life. Christianity is not only about what you believe, but what you do. You can say you believe, but if you don't do it, then you are deceived. James will tell us in a later passage that even demons have correct theology, but obviously, they are not saved. People can say they believe in the Bible but if they don't obey it, then they don't believe in it.

Jesus told a parable about a house that was built on a rock compared to a house that was built on sand. When a storm came, the one built on the rock stood firm, but the one built on sand collapsed. The houses represented a person's life. One person built their life on sand, the other on rock. They both listened to the Word of God. The difference? Jesus said, He who hears the word and does it, is compared to someone who built their house on a rock. The person who hears the word and doesn't do it is one who built their house on sand. (Matthew 7:24-29)

One philosophy has led more to this problem than any other in our postmodern culture —relativism. Relativism says what is true for you may not be true for me. Relativism is often shaped by pragmatism, which says that truth is whatever works for me. Whatever works best for us becomes our truth. The modern church approaches the Bible in the same way. We ask the question, "What does that verse mean to you?" We allow our interpretation of the Scriptures to be relative.

But that is the wrong way to approach the Scripture. The authors who wrote the Biblical passages had a specific agenda and an intended meaning when they wrote what they did. Our task is not to make it say what we want it to say, but to discover what the author meant. From there, we can discover the universal principles, and apply the meaning to our particular situation.

With a relativistic approach, we don't obey the Word because if we don't like what it says, we change the meaning. In that way, our conscience is relieved and we feel that we have "obeyed" God's word. But if that is how we approach the Scriptures, then we are deceived. Remember, the Bible is not an answer book. It is a wisdom book. It shows us the right way to live, but then we need to live that way. If we do, we will receive God's blessing; if not, the word will become lifeless to us.

> *But prove yourselves doers of the word, and not merely hearers who delude themselves. For if anyone is a hearer of the word and not a doer, he is like a man who looks at his natural face in a mirror; for once he has looked at himself and gone away, he has immediately forgotten what kind of person he was. But one who looks intently at the perfect law, the law of liberty, and abides by it, not having become a forgetful hearer but an effectual doer, this man will be blessed in what he does. (James 1:22-25)*

Reflection Questions:

1. Mark Twain once said it's not the parts of the Bible he doesn't understand that bothers him. It's the parts he does understand. Can you relate to that? Can you think of any areas of your life where you know the Bible says to behave in a certain way, but you are not doing it?

2. If so, what are the reasons that are holding you back?

3. What adjustments could you make in your life, or what would need to change to move toward obedience?

James 1:26-27

vs.26-27—If anyone thinks himself to be religious, and yet does not bridle his tongue but deceives his own heart, this man's religion is worthless. Pure and undefiled religion in the sight of our God and Father is this: to visit orphans and widows in their distress, and to keep oneself unstained by the world.

James uses the word *"religion"* three times. Many see religion as a bad thing, but it doesn't have to be. James compares true religion and false religion. He identifies false religion in five ways.

1) False religion is worthless—*"this man's religion is worthless."* Worthless means it has no value. There may be a lot of activity, but it is meaningless.

2) False religion is sincere—*"if anyone thinks himself to be religious."* People who follow empty religion believe in their false system of faith. Look at the sincerity of the people Jesus spoke about in Matthew 7:21-23.

> *"Not everyone who says to Me, 'Lord, Lord,' will enter the kingdom of heaven, but he who does the will of My Father who is in heaven will enter. Many will say to Me on that day, 'Lord, Lord, did we not prophesy in Your name, and in Your name cast out demons, and in Your name perform many miracles?' And then I will declare to them, 'I never knew you; depart from Me, you who practice lawlessness.'*

3) False religion is active—*"If anyone thinks himself to be religious."* This person thinks he or she is religious because of his or her activities: prayer, reading Bible, attending church, feeding the hungry, charitable works, etc. There is danger here because true religion does require activity, but the empty shell of activity can deceive us.

4) False religion is deceptive—*"deceives his own heart."* These people are not intentionally hypocrites. It's just that all their activities trick them into thinking their faith is legitimate. Jesus addressed just such a group in Revelation, chapter three. *To the angel of the church in Sardis write: He who has the seven Spirits of God and the seven stars, says this: 'I know*

your deeds, that you have a name that you are alive, but you are dead. (Revelation 3:1)

5) False religion is contaminated—*"Pure and undefiled religion."* James speaks of true religion as being *"pure and undefiled."* That implies that worthless religion is not pure, but contaminated. Worthless religion moves us away from the simplicity of Christ. (2 Corinthians 11:3) How? By adding all kinds of man-made ideas.

James contrasts that with three aspects of true religion.

1) God sets the standard with true religion—*"In the sight of our God."* In other words, we could word it this way, "True religion, as far as God is concerned, is…" True religion is what God says it is, not what we think it is.

2) True religion flows out of family ties, not organizational structure—*"Pure and undefiled religion in the sight of our God and Father is this."* Here James refers to God as our *"Father."* Religious practice is always connected to the fact that we are in relationship with God. That's what Christians mean when they say they're not into religion, but into a relationship. We engage in devotion and spiritual activity, not as an end in themselves, but because we love God who is our heavenly Father.

3) True religion is a matter of the heart—*"Pure and undefiled religion in the sight of our God…"* The word *"pure"* is a Greek term (kithara) that is used in the New Testament to refer to purity of heart. True religion focuses on the condition of a person's heart. The heart condition is seen through three life patterns. These patterns that James lists, are representative, not exhaustive.

1) Personal restraint—*"If anyone thinks himself to be religious, and yet does not bridle his tongue…"* The tongue reveals what is in the heart.

2) Social compassion—*"…to visit orphans and widows in their distress…"* It is interesting the people groups James picks; orphans and widows were the most vulnerable in that society. There were no safety nets or government programs to help the most vulnerable. This is about reaching out to those on the margins of society.

3) Moral purity—*"…and to keep oneself unstained by the world."*

Reflection Questions:

1. Thinking over the three life patterns of true religion—personal restraint, social compassion and moral purity—in which area are you the strongest?

2. Which area could use a tune up?

3. What steps could you take to make any needed course corrections?

James 2:1-3

vs.1-3—My brethren, do not hold your faith in our glorious Lord Jesus Christ with an attitude of personal favoritism. For if a man comes into your assembly with a gold ring and dressed in fine clothes, and there also comes in a poor man in dirty clothes, and you pay special attention to the one who is wearing the fine clothes, and say, "You sit here in a good place," and you say to the poor man, "You stand over there, or sit down by my footstool,"

James mentions *"personal favoritism."* It's one word in the Greek, but it literally means "to seek the face of another." It has come to describe one who is attracted to one person over another based on external judgments. It's about giving preference to someone based on race, popularity, influence or wealth. In this situation James is speaking specifically about pandering to the rich. *"For if a man comes into your assembly with a gold ring and dressed in fine clothes, and there also comes in a poor man in dirty clothes, and you pay special attention to the one who is wearing the fine clothes, and say, 'You sit here in a good place,' and you say to the poor man, 'You stand over there, or sit down by my footstool'" (James 2:2-3)*

Don't think this doesn't happen today. Who gets more of the pastor's attention, the person who depends on welfare, or the person who is a powerful member of the community? I have been a pastor for over 35 years. There were times in the past, when I was pressured to cater to a group's personal desires because they were the one's who most heavily supported the church.

This kind of prejudice has been horribly destructive. Mahatma Gandhi wrote in his autobiography that during his student days he read the Gospels seriously and considered converting to Christianity. He believed that in the teachings of Jesus he could find the solution to the caste system that was dividing the people of India. So one Sunday he decided to attend services at a nearby church and talk to the minister about becoming a Christian. When he entered the sanctuary, however, the usher refused to give him a seat and suggested that he go worship with his own people. Gandhi left the church and never returned. "If Christians have caste differences also, I might as well remain a Hindu," he reasoned. That usher's prejudice not only betrayed Jesus but also turned a person away from trusting Him as Savior.[11]

Reflection Questions:

1. In what ways do you see evidence of personal favoritism in your behavior, family or church?

2. Racial tensions are real in America. Do you think that is due in large to white insensitivity, or black over-sensitivity, or something else?

3. In what ways have prejudices touched your life?

---

[11] Our Daily Bread, March 6, 1994

James 2:4

v.4—have you not made distinctions among yourselves, and become judges with evil motives?

James is asking this question in a rhetorical way. In other words, this is precisely what we are doing when we show personal favoritism. To *"make distinctions"* is in contrast to *"having faith in the Lord." (James 2:1)* You can't have faith in Jesus and make personal distinctions, because it goes against our understanding that we are all equally in need of salvation. No one is more or less deserving of grace than another.

Personal favoritism says something about our understanding of the gospel. It apportions value and merit to the human condition. But at the cross we are all equal. To judge people, based on their color, or economic status makes distinctions that say one group needs more grace than another; which means that one group is "better" than another.

The unspoken implication is that Christ doesn't need to rescue the "better" group as completely. At that point we have devalued the sacrifice of Christ. Certainly people don't think this through, so they don't realize what they are doing. Instead, their motives are simply selfish. James says they *"judge with evil motives."* They are seeking personal advantage. In this case, it is financial advantage.

When we show favoritism or prejudice, we are cutting at the heart of the gospel. Frederick Douglass wrote a scathing indictment on American religion:

> Indeed, I can see no reason, but the most deceitful one, for calling the religion of this land Christianity. I look upon it as the climax of all misnomers, the boldest of all frauds, and the grossest of all libels. Never was there a clearer case of "stealing the livery of the court of heaven to serve the devil in." I am filled with unutterable loathing when I contemplate the religious pomp and show, together with the horrible inconsistencies, which every where surround me. We have men-stealers for ministers, women-whippers for missionaries, and cradle-plunderers for church members.

> The man who wields the blood-clotted cowskin during the week fills the pulpit on Sunday, and claims to be a minister of the meek and lowly Jesus. The man who robs me of my earnings at the end of each week meets me as a class-leader on Sunday morning, to show me the way of life, and the path of salvation. He who sells my sister, for purposes of prostitution, stands forth as the pious advocate of purity.[12]

Prejudice in any form is something to avoid at all costs, for Paul says if someone preaches a different gospel, *"Let him be accursed!" (Galatians 1:8; 2 Corinthians 11:4)* That's something to think about!

Reflection Questions:

1. Personal bias or prejudice is actually preaching a different gospel. What reasons do you think James or the other apostles would make that assertion?

2. James speaks against making distinctions, yet slavery was practiced in that day. How can we reconcile the Bible's silence on that subject with Paul's statements that in Christ there is neither male nor female, slave nor free?

3. Aside from treating people unfairly, what is the nature of the sin of favoritism or racism?

4. If you can you identify areas in your life where you have made distinctions between yourself and others, what were the motives behind your attitudes or behaviors?

---

[12] *Global Voices On Biblical Equality: Men and Women Ministering Together In the Church*, Edited by Aida Besancon Spencer and William David Spencer, Mimi Haddad, Eugene, OR: Wipf and Stock Publishers, 2008, Kindle, 377.

James 2:5-7

vs.5-7—Listen, my beloved brethren: did not God choose the poor of this world to be rich in faith and heirs of the kingdom which He promised to those who love Him? But you have dishonored the poor man. Is it not the rich who oppress you and personally drag you into court? Do they not blaspheme the fair name by which you have been called?

James makes some pretty drastic statements about the poor and the rich. It sounds like he's anti-rich, but that's not really the case. These are generalizations. He's not saying all poor are righteous, nor is he saying that all rich are evil. But generally, the poor are more likely to come to Christ. Monika Hellwig in *Christianity Today,* gives ten reasons Why.

1. The poor know they are in urgent need of redemption.
2. The poor know not only their dependence on God and on powerful people but also their interdependence with one another.
3. The poor rest their security not on things but on people.
4. The poor have no exaggerated sense of their own importance, and no exaggerated need of privacy.
5. The poor expect little from competition and much from cooperation.
6. The poor can distinguish between necessities and luxuries.
7. The poor can wait, because they have acquired a kind of dogged patience born of acknowledged dependence.
8. The fears of the poor are more realistic and less exaggerated, because they already know that one can survive great suffering and want.
9. When the poor have the Gospel preached to them, it sounds like good news and not like a threat or a scolding.
10. The poor can respond to the call of the Gospel with a certain abandonment and uncomplicated totality because they have so little to lose and are ready for anything.[13]

Generally, the rich are more likely not to come to Christ. The Apostle Paul tells us why that's the case.

---

[13] Monika Hellwig, *Christianity Today, November 13, 1995.*

> *6 But godliness actually is a means of great gain when accompanied by contentment. 7 For we have brought nothing into the world, so we cannot take anything out of it either. 8 If we have food and covering, with these we shall be content. 9 But those who want to get rich fall into temptation and a snare and many foolish and harmful desires which plunge men into ruin and destruction. 10 For the love of money is a root of all sorts of evil, and some by longing for it have wandered away from the faith and pierced themselves with many griefs. (1 Timothy 6:6-10)*

Specifically in the situation James was referring to, the poor had no recourse in that society to call for justice in the courts, but the rich were able to file complaints against the poor. Often the rich took advantage of the poor. James is saying a poor person certainly will not do that to you, but if anyone does do that to you, it will be the rich because the poor couldn't.

Based on James' statement, one might wonder, is it evil to make a lot of money? No. God prospers people so they can give to the poor. The fact that people are starving all over the world is not because God isn't supplying the money or food. It's because of the fact that God has supplied both the money and the food through His people around the world, but they aren't releasing it.

The attitude we should have toward wealth was expressed by Paul in Philippians 4:12-13:

> *12 I know how to get along with humble means, and I also know how to live in prosperity; in any and every circumstance I have learned the secret of being filled and going hungry, both of having abundance and suffering need. 13 I can do all things through Him who strengthens me.*

Notice, no matter if he is rich or poor, his source and his dependence is on Christ.

Reflection Questions:

1. When you face a financial difficulty, is your first response to turn to your credit card, or to pray?

2. Wealth is a relative term. People in America who make $30,000 a year or less are considered poor. But that much money would be a fortune in some parts of the world. In light of that reality, do you think American Christians have a greater obligation to give than do those less fortunate?

3. What kinds of practical changes could you make to free up more funds to give to those in need?

James 2:8-13

vs. 8-13— If, however, you are fulfilling the royal law according to the Scripture, "You shall love your neighbor as yourself," you are doing well. But if you show partiality, you are committing sin and are convicted by the law as transgressors. For whoever keeps the whole law and yet stumbles in one point, he has become guilty of all. For He who said, "DO not commit adultery," also said, "DO not commit murder." Now if you do not commit adultery, but do commit murder, you have become a transgressor of the law. So speak and so act as those who are to be judged by the law of liberty. For judgment will be merciless to one who has shown no mercy; mercy triumphs over judgment.

Jesus emphasized that law:

> *Teacher, which is the great commandment in the Law?" And He said to him, "'YOU SHALL LOVE THE LORD YOUR GOD WITH ALL YOUR HEART, AND WITH ALL YOUR SOUL, AND WITH ALL YOUR MIND.' "This is the great and foremost commandment. "The second is like it, 'YOU SHALL LOVE YOUR NEIGHBOR AS YOURSELF.' "On these two commandments depend the whole Law and the Prophets. (Matthew 22:36-40)*

We obviously can't love others like we love ourselves if we show partiality. *"But if you show partiality, you are committing sin and are convicted by the law as transgressors." (James 2:9)* Preferential treatment, the "good ol' boy system" and prejudice are clearly identified as sin.

"For whoever keeps the whole law and yet stumbles in one point, he has become guilty of all. For He who said, 'DO NOT COMMIT ADULTERY,' also said, 'DO NOT COMMIT MURDER.' Now if you do not commit adultery, but do commit murder, you have become a transgressor of the law." (James 2:10-11) To break the law of love is to break all of God's law. Selfishness and personal favoritism are serious offenses. In God's eyes they are grouped with adultery and murder. *"So speak and so act as those who are to be judged by the law of liberty. For judgment will be*

merciless to one who has shown no mercy; mercy triumphs over judgment." (James 2:12-13)

This is a harsh statement, but what James is saying is, the way we treat people based on external conditions reveals the true nature of our profession. If we show favoritism, and do not repent once shown our error, then we're not really in the faith. That person will receive no mercy from God.

Reflection Questions:

1. What reasons can you think of that God would deem personal favoritism and prejudice such serious offenses?

2. Can you recall a time when you were judged or slighted because of favoritism or prejudice? If so, what were your thoughts or emotions at the time?

3. Can you recall a time when you treated others with prejudice or favoritism?

4. In what ways can you be more sensitive to this issue?

James 2:14

***v.14—What use is it, my brethren, if someone says he has faith but he has no works?
Can that faith save him?***

James has been laying down the tests of an authentic faith. First we saw that one's faith is authenticated by their reaction to trials. Now James raises the next test in authenticating one's faith. John Calvin wrote, "It is faith alone that justifies, but faith that justifies is never alone." That's the difference between a living faith and a dead faith.

James begins this section with a rhetorical question. *"What use is it, my brethren, if someone says he has faith but he has no works?" (James 2:14a)* In other words, faith without works has no use. And yet, this person is professing to have faith—*"If someone says he has faith."*

What they mean by that can be seen back in verse one. *"My brethren, do not hold your faith in our glorious Lord Jesus Christ with an attitude of personal favoritism." (James 2:1)* This person is professing to *"hold faith"* in Jesus Christ. They are saying they believe in Christ; that they are a Christian. Yet, the faith they profess is useless. That's the point of James' question—*"what use is it?"*

James then asks, *"Can that faith save him?" (James 2:14b)* This is also a rhetorical question, so the obvious answer is "No". "Workless" faith cannot save. That sounds like salvation by works. That was Martin Luther's problem with this passage. But that was not the point James was making. We are saved by faith, but if faith is real, there will be evidence. A professed faith without evidence is a false faith. If we truly believe, it will change the way we live.

Reflection Questions:

1. In what ways can you see a difference in your life since you became a follower of Jesus Christ?

2. I once heard someone say that once you become a Christian you can do anything you want to do. However, once you are a Christian, your

"want-tos" will change. In what ways have you noticed a change in your desires or motives since becoming a Christian?

3. If you have been a Christian for most of your life, there is little to compare with your life "before Christ." However, the presence of Jesus in a human heart produces grace and mercy. In what ways do you see a growing tendency to extend grace and mercy toward others, or is this quality lacking in your life?

James 2:15-17

vs.15-17—If a brother or sister is without clothing and in need of daily food, and one of you says to them, "Go in peace, be warmed and be filled," and yet you do not give them what is necessary for their body, what use is that? Even so faith, if it has no works, is dead, being by itself.

James has just said that faith must be evidenced by works. Now he will explain what he means. *"If a brother or sister is without clothing and in need of daily food, and one of you says to them, 'Go in peace, be warmed and be filled,' and yet you do not give them what is necessary for their body, what use is that?" (James 2:15)* The statement to *"Go in peace, be warmed and be filled,"* is in the passive voice in the Greek. That means the statement could be interpreted "Let someone else feed and warm you." The speaker has no intention of doing it. The implication is that he or she will remember the needy individual to God when in prayer. It's the—"I'll pray for you"—comment, when what they need is a helping hand.

In this case, intercession is more than saying words. It's getting involved. Belief that is divorced from action is useless. *"Even so faith, if it has no works, is dead, being by itself." (James 2:17)* This is the kind of faith that accompanies the church at Sardis. *"You have a name that you are alive, but you are dead." (Revelation 3:1)*

In the last verse of this chapter, James will make the analogy of the body and spirit with faith and works. *"For just as the body without the spirit is dead, so also faith without works is dead." (James 2:26)* Death is a severing from environment. When the spirit leaves the body, the body is dead. The spirit inside the body that animated the body is gone, so the body is dead. Likewise, James is saying the works that animated the faith is gone, so the faith is dead. It has no power to save.

That means that people who say they believe in Jesus, but have no works, are in actuality, lost. Why?: Because faith is the means of new life, the life of Jesus. And if the life of Jesus is in us, then that will result in compassion. So when we see someone in need, we are compelled to help him or her, not because we want to earn salvation, but because our possession of salvation compels us to help others.

Reflection Questions:

1. In what ways are you involved in serving others?

2. What is your true motivation for serving the Lord?

3. What talents or skills do you possess that could be of service to God's Kingdom?

4. If you could be involved in any ministry and not fail, what would you do?

James 2:18

v.18—But someone may well say, "You have faith and I have works"; show me your faith without the works, and I will show you my faith by my works.

James has just laid down the proposition that real faith will be evidenced by works. He imagines someone offering an objection, so he role-plays that conversation. *"But someone may well say, 'You have faith and I have works'" (James 2:18a)* This person is seeing faith and works as two separate things. One person has faith, and the other person has works. The implication is that works are fine, but just because works are absent, that doesn't mean the faith is not authentic.

But James challenges this kind of thinking. *"Show me your faith without the works" (James 2:18b)* In other words, prove you have faith. How do you know you have faith if you can't see it? Do you know you have it because you say you know what you believe? How do you prove an intangible belief without tangible evidence? Is faith simply an intellectual set of ideas?

What James is getting at, is that faith is not simply a set of beliefs. Faith is not seen by what one believes, but it is seen by what one does. *"And I will show you my faith by my works." (James 2:18c)* You can only see faith through action. We are saved by faith alone, but faith that is real will change how we live. If there is no change, then the faith wasn't real.

Jesus told the story of a father with two sons. The father asked the sons to go work in the field. The first son said he would do it, but later changed his mind and didn't go. The second son said he didn't want to go, but later changed his mind and went to the field. Jesus then asked the crowd who did the will of the father. The people answered, the son who actually went into the field. (Matthew 21:28-32) The first son professed obedience, but it was hallow. It was the son who acted that actually obeyed. So it is with faith. We can confess what we believe, but what we truly believe is evidenced by what we do, not what we say.

Reflection Questions:

1. In what ways do you see evidence for your faith?

2. In what ways do your measure the growth of your faith?

3. If our faith is on the 50-yard line, what actions could you take to move it down field five yards?

James 2:19-20

vs.19-20—You believe that God is one. You do well; the demons also believe, and shudder. But are you willing to recognize, you foolish fellow, that faith without works is useless?

James has been making the argument that correct belief alone will not save. He now gives an extreme example of that. *"You believe that God is one." (James 2:19a)* This was the central tenant of Judaism. They believed in monotheism, the truth that there is only one God. Every day, devout Jews still recite the creedal declaration of Israel—*"Hear O Israel, the Lord thy God, the Lord is One God." (Deuteronomy 6:4)* James mentions this to represent all their theological beliefs. In essence he was saying their theology was correct. But from that, they were making an assumption; that correct theology meant they possessed a living faith. But that was an incorrect assumption, so James proceeded to correct their thinking.

"You do well the demons also believe." (James 2:19b) The first thing you need to notice here is that James says—*"you do well."* That means the correct understanding of God is important, but it's not enough. You can't be saved without a right understanding of Jesus Christ, but a right understanding of Jesus Christ by itself is not enough to be saved. James makes that point by showing us the absurdity of depending on theology alone—*"the demons also believe."*

If you think about it, there's no such thing as a liberal demon. They are not atheists, or agnostics. They know God exists. They believe in the deity of Jesus of Nazareth. They believe in the virgin birth. They believe in the Trinity. They believe in the death of Christ on the cross for the sins of the world. They believe in the resurrection. They believe in the 2nd coming of Jesus Christ. The demons know who Jesus is. *"Just then there was a man in their synagogue with an unclean spirit; and he cried out, saying, 'What business do we have with each other, Jesus of Nazareth? Have You come to destroy us? I know who You are—the Holy One of God!'" (Mark 1:23-24)*

Demons have correct theology, but they are lost. Why?: Because correct theology alone is not enough to save. And not only do they have correct theology; they have deep emotion to support it. *"The demons also believe and shudder." (James 2:19c)* That word shudder means to bristle, to have the hair stand on end. Demons are in a high degree of terror. They are emotionally stirred by the presence of Jesus, but they are still lost.

In order to be saved, we have to believe the right things, and our hearts must be engaged, but correct theology and strong emotional reactions to Jesus are still not enough to be saved. Saving faith is intellectual, and emotional, but also volitional. *"But are you willing to recognize, you foolish fellow, that faith without works is useless?" (James 2:20)*

He's saying, don't be foolish. Belief alone won't save. Emotion won't save. Your faith must include your will. When you give your whole will to God, it will affect your behavior. True faith will result in works.

Reflection Questions:

1. Like the question about the chicken and the egg, which comes first, faith or works?

2. What is the difference between what James is teaching and a works theology?

3. If people do a lot of good deeds, is that enough to claim salvation, or is something more required?

James 2:21

v. 21—Was not Abraham our father justified by works when he offered up Isaac his son on the altar?

Theologians have wrestled with this part of James, because it seems to directly contradict what the apostle Paul wrote.

> *For we maintain that a man is justified by faith apart from works of the Law. (Romans 3:28)*

> *Nevertheless knowing that a man is not justified by the works of the Law but through faith in Christ Jesus, (Galatians 2:16)*

> *For by grace you have been saved through faith; and that not of yourselves, it is the gift of God; not as a result of works, so that no one may boast. (Ephesians 2:8-9)*

A careful reading of the New Testament shows that James and Paul were not in conflict. When Paul began to preach the gospel, James was the leader of the Jerusalem church. Paul submitted his gospel to the leaders of the church for their examination. *"It was because of a revelation that I went up; and I submitted to them the gospel which I preach among the Gentiles, but I did so in private to those who were of reputation, for fear that I might be running, or had run, in vain." (Galatians 2:2)* After he presented what he was preaching, he shared his assessment of their response. *"But from those who were of high reputation (what they were makes no difference to me; God shows no partiality)—well, those who were of reputation contributed nothing to me." (Galatians 2:6)* In other words, they didn't add anything to what he was preaching. His message was acknowledged by the church leadership to be accurate.

But notice who sat on the church council, *"...and recognizing the grace that had been given to me, James and Cephas and John, who were reputed to be pillars, gave to me and Barnabas the right hand of fellowship, so that we might go to the Gentiles and they to the circumcised." (Galatians 2:9)* James, the leader of the church, heard Paul's gospel and approved of it. Paul's gospel was clearly that salvation came by grace through faith alone, and James agreed with that truth. But Paul also believed that faith must demonstrate itself through works.

> *For in Christ Jesus neither circumcision nor uncircumcision means anything, but faith working through love. (Galatians 5:6)*
>
> *For we are His workmanship, created in Christ Jesus for good works, which God prepared beforehand so that we would walk in them. (Ephesians 2:10)*
>
> *Who gave Himself for us to redeem us from every lawless deed, and to purify for Himself a people for His own possession, zealous for good deeds. (Titus 2:14)*
>
> *This is a trustworthy statement; and concerning these things I want you to speak confidently, so that those who have believed God will be careful to engage in good deeds. These things are good and profitable for men. (Titus 3:8)*

Paul and James agreed in doctrine. But James' statement here, and Paul's statement about Abraham sound completely contradictory. James wrote:

> *Was not Abraham our father justified by works—v.21*
>
> *You see that a man is justified by works and not by faith alone—v.24*

But here's what Paul wrote:

> *For if Abraham was justified by works, he has something to boast about, but not before God. For what does the Scripture say? "ABRAHAM BELIEVED GOD, AND IT WAS CREDITED TO HIM AS RIGHTEOUSNESS." Now to the one who works, his wage is not credited as a favor, but as what is due. But to the one who does not work, but believes in Him who justifies the ungodly, his faith is credited as righteousness. (Romans 4:2-5)*

It sounds like Paul is saying the exact opposite of what James said. However, when we read the two passages in their context, we see that Paul and James are referring to two different times in Abraham's life. Paul refers to the initial justification of Abraham in Genesis 15 when he believed God's promise in the face of impossibility. James is referring to what happened in Genesis 22 when Abraham offered Isaac on the altar. *"Was not Abraham our father justified by works when he offered up Isaac his son on the altar?" (James 2:21)* Abraham was justified in Genesis 15 by his faith, but his works in Genesis 22 were the fruit and outward evidence of his faith that had begun back in Genesis 15.

Reflection Questions:

1. Hopefully, you can see how easy it would be to pull Scripture verses out of context to make them say something completely different than the author intended. In your devotional reading, do you tend to parachute into a passage, or do you read all the verses in the "neighborhood" in order to establish context?

2. In what ways would your Bible study habits change if you were committed to understanding the context of a passage?

3. Do you have specific Bible study goals? If so, what are they? If not, why not consider making some?

James 2:22-26

vs.22-26—You see that faith was working with his works, and as a result of the works, faith was perfected; and the Scripture was fulfilled which says, "And Abraham believed God, and it was reckoned to him as righteousness," and he was called the friend of God. You see that a man is justified by works and not by faith alone. In the same way, was not Rahab the harlot also justified by works when she received the messengers and sent them out by another way? For just as the body without the spirit is dead, so also faith without works is dead.

James is talking about how faith and works go together—*"You see that faith was working with his works, and as a result of the works, faith was perfected." (v.22)* The word *"perfection"* means "to bring something to its conclusion" or "to bring it to fruition." James is not saying that faith is insufficient to save, but rather, that saving faith has an intended goal; good works. Edmond Heibert, in his commentary on James wrote, "James is saying that the belief God accepted as righteousness in Genesis 15 [when God first called Abraham] must ultimately manifest itself in the unquestioning obedience described in Genesis 22 [when Abraham sacrificed Isaac]."[14]

In thus testing Abraham's faith, God brought into manifestation the reality of faith he knew was already there. And that's the kind of faith God will receive. (James 2:23-24) James then builds on his point by using another Biblical example. *"In the same way, was not Rahab the harlot also justified by works when she received the messengers and sent them out by another way? For just as the body without the spirit is dead, so also faith without works is dead." (James 2:25-26)* James introduces Rahab who was about as opposite of Abraham as you could get: He is male. She is female. He's a Jew. She's a Gentile. He's a patriarch. She's a prostitute. Yet she too was saved by faith, and that faith expressed itself through works.

Commenting on this, John Calvin wrote, "He designedly put together two persons so different in their character, in order more clearly to show, that no one, whatever may have been his or her condition, nation, or class in

---

[14] D. Edmond Heibert, James, rev. ed., BMH Books, 2002.

society, has ever been counted righteous without good works."[15] Notice Calvin didn't say they were made righteous by good works, but rather they were accounted righteous. In other words, we are not made righteous by our works; we are made righteous by faith. But, we demonstrate the reality of that righteousness by good works. James' final solution ends where he began—*"Faith without works is dead."*

Reflection Questions:

1. In what ways has your faith in Jesus Christ changed the way you live?

2. What works do you see in your life that has resulted because of your faith?

3. In what ways can you demonstrate that your faith is real?

---

[15] C. J. Mahaney, *Sermon Quotes: "Got Faith?"*, Sovereign Grace Church of Louisville, 2016, Accessed 2019, https://www.sgclouisville.org/from-the-pastors/post/sermon-quotes--got-faith-.

James 3:1-5a

> *vs.1-5a—Let not many of you become teachers, my brethren, knowing that as such we will incur a stricter judgment. For we all stumble in many ways. If anyone does not stumble in what he says, he is a perfect man, able to bridle the whole body as well. Now if we put the bits into the horses' mouths so that they will obey us, we direct their entire body as well. Look at the ships also, though they are so great and are driven by strong winds, are still directed by a very small rudder wherever the inclination of the pilot desires. So also the tongue is a small part of the body, and yet it boasts of great things.*

So far in our study we have seen that James has been dealing with the tests of an authentic faith. An authentic faith is seen in: how we respond to trials, how we respond to the Word of God, in the quality of our religion, in how we treat others who are different than us and through our good works. The next test of an authentic faith is the test of the tongue. God will judge the authenticity of our faith, by how we talk, because our words reveal the true condition of our heart. James will start the examination of the tongue by looking at teachers. *"Let not many of you become teachers, my brethren, knowing that as such we will incur a stricter judgment." (James 3:1)*

The word *"judgment"* is generic. It's not referring to one of the specific future judgments, but the judgment of whether or not the teacher's faith is real. God is going to assess (judge) the authenticity of the teacher's faith by his or her words—privately, as with everyone, but even more so publicly.

For the teacher, there's a higher standard to determine if their faith is real, because the nature of their calling is to speak for God. A teacher's speech is the heart of who they are. So for them to fail to accurately and obediently teach God's word is to deny the Lord whom they say they serve.

Is there room for slipping up? Sure. *"For we all stumble in many ways. If anyone does not stumble in what he says, he is a perfect man, able to bridle the whole body as well." (James 3:2)* James is saying that everyone sins with the tongue, even teachers. But the maturity of one who is able to teach can be determined by the use of their tongue. So yes, teachers do sin with their mouth, but when we do we repent, change our behavior and move forward.

This is vital because teachers have such a powerful influence on the Body of Christ. James expresses the power a teacher possesses.

> *Now if we put the bits into the horses' mouths so that they will obey us, we direct their entire body as well. Look at the ships also, though they are so great and are driven by strong winds, are still directed by a very small rudder wherever the inclination of the pilot desires. So also the tongue is a small part of the body, and yet it boasts of great things. (James 3:3-5a)*

To be a teacher you are signing up to be God's spokesperson. As such, your faith is then measured not only by your private speech, but also, by whether you are an obedient spokesperson. What are the criteria of an obedient teacher of the word?

1. They live what they teach
2. They practice proper hermeneutics:
    a. The context of the time it was written.
    b. The purpose for which it was written.
    c. An analysis of the original language.
    d. Faithful to literary context.
    e. Faithful to the kind of literature.
3. They apply the Biblical truth to our culture and lives.
4. They always interpret the Bible through the one lens that is above all: the grand theme of the Bible is Jesus.

Reflection Questions:

1. What are the criteria you use when picking a teacher/preacher to sit under?

2. Would you lean more towards being a person who wants to be taught, or to be inspired?

3. Interesting, entertaining and inspiring teaching is great. There is nothing wrong with wanting to sit under that kind of ministry. But if

the teacher does not handle the Word accurately, would you be willing to seek for one who does?

James 3:5b

v.5b—See how great a forest is set aflame by such a small fire!

In the last lesson we saw that teachers are responsible for what they say because their tongues have great influence. Now James will apply the lesson to everyone. He will take the next section and focus on the potentially destructive power of the tongue. Water can't multiply. A cup of water won't become a flood. But with a match, you can burn down a forest.

Proverbs 26 speaks of a person causing division with the tongue. The writer identifies four characteristics of someone who sins with their tongue.

1. They perpetuate division and contention. *"For lack of wood the fire goes out, and where there is no whisperer, contention quiets down." (Proverbs 26:20)* The word *"whisperer"* refers to one who murmurs, criticizes, grumbles or slanders. If just those four things stopped, there would be no fighting in churches.

2. Their words are inviting and persuasive. *"The words of a whisperer are like dainty morsels, and they go down into the innermost parts of the body." (Proverbs 26:22)* The phrase, *"dainty morsels"* is from a Hebrew word that means to swallow greedily. It's no surprise people love gossip. Their ears perk up the moment someone starts to speak about another person, especially if they talk in whispered tones. Standing in the grocery story isle makes that abundantly clear with a proliferation of gossip magazines inviting us to take up and read.

3. They disguise a wicked heart. *"Like an earthen vessel overlaid with silver dross are burning lips and a wicked heart. He who hates disguises it with his lips, but he lays up deceit in his heart. When he speaks graciously, do not believe him, for there are seven abominations in his heart. Though his hatred covers itself with guile, his wickedness will be revealed before the assembly." (Proverbs 26:23-26)*

4. They sound innocent, but their intent is to destroy. *"A lying tongue hates those it crushes, and a flattering mouth works ruin." (Proverbs*

26:28) In light of who we are as believers, gossip and contentious speech should have no place in a Christian's life. Paul makes this clear in Ephesians, chapter four. *"Let no unwholesome word proceed from your mouth, but only such a word as is good for edification according to the need of the moment, so that it will give grace to those who hear." (Ephesians 4:29)*

The word *"unwholesome"* refers to rotting fruit. It is a picture of something that is decaying. These would be words that dismantle someone; casting of doubt here, creating suspicion there. It's the opposite of building up. Paul is saying unless our words are constructive, they shouldn't be uttered. It's like the old cliché our mothers taught us: If you can't say something nice, don't say anything at all. In fact, Paul offers specific criteria for acceptable speech, in regards to speaking about others.

1. Our words need to build others up—*"only such a word as is good for edification."*
2. Our words need to be timely—*"according to the need of the moment."*
3. Our words need to be empowering—*"that it might give grace."*
4. Our words need to be focused on those present—*"to those who hear."*

Reflection Questions:

1. In what ways would your relationships change if you adhered strictly to Paul's admonition?

2. Can you recall the last conversation you had where you built up someone else? Describe what happened.

3. If someone in your circle begins to gossip about another person, what could you say to help steer the conversation in another direction?

James 3:6

v.6—And the tongue is a fire, the very world of iniquity; the tongue is set among our members as that which defiles the entire body, and sets on fire the course of our life, and is set on fire by hell.

James is talking about the destructive nature of the tongue. He refers to it as *"the very world of iniquity."* Iniquity refers to an absence of moral or spiritual values, morally objectionable behavior, or injustice. James is saying an entire system of evil is bound up within the tongue, waiting to escape into the world. There's an organized crime syndicate in our mouths because the tongue can give expression to every evil thought and motive. The mouth is the doorway to great sin. *"The tongue is set among our members as that which defiles the entire body."* A filthy tongue results in a filthy person.

Jesus explained how it works:

> *But the things that proceed out of the mouth come from the heart, and those defile the man. For out of the heart come evil thoughts, murders, adulteries, fornications, thefts, false witness, slanders. These are the things which defile the man; but to eat with unwashed hands does not defile the man. (Matthew 15:18-20)*

What you say can defile you. But Jesus equates what you say with what you do. *"But the things that proceed out of the mouth…those defile the man"* (v.18) Jesus then lists a number of deeds: *"evil thoughts, murders, adulteries, fornications, thefts, false witness, slanders"* (v.19) But then notice what he says about those deeds in verse 20. *"These are the things which defile the man."*

This means a person is defiled both by what he or she says and by what he or she does. The reason is because both things stem from the heart.

> *v.18—"But the things that proceed out of the mouth <u>come from the heart</u>."*

> *v.19—"<u>For out of the heart</u> come evil thoughts, murders, adulteries, fornications, thefts, false witness, slanders."*

All this sin originates from the heart and is expressed through the mouth, and when it's expressed through the mouth it reinforces what's in the heart, so that eventually what's in the heart is not only expressed through our speech, but carried out with our body. In that way our speech can defile us.

Reflection Questions:

1. Our words have the power to shape what we become. Keeping that in mind, and thinking about your patterns of speech, what type of person are you becoming?

2. Thinking about the kind of person you would like to become, what kind of speech should you practice?

3. What changes do you need to make in your speech to alter the trajectory of your development?

James 3:6b-12

vs. 6b-12—and sets on fire the course of our life, and is set on fire by hell. For every species of beasts and birds, of reptiles and creatures of the sea, is tamed and has been tamed by the human race. But no one can tame the tongue; it is a restless evil and full of deadly poison. With it we bless our Lord and Father, and with it we curse men, who have been made in the likeness of God; from the same mouth come both blessing and cursing. My brethren, these things ought not to be this way. Does a fountain send out from the same opening both fresh and bitter water? Can a fig tree, my brethren, produce olives, or a vine produce figs? Nor can salt water produce fresh.

The tongue's influence spreads to the entire life. Notice the progression. First James describes it as a system of wickedness. Then he talks about how it defiles the whole person. Then finally, he says it sets ablaze the entire course of a person's life. The phrase James uses for this description of the tongue—*"the course of our life"*—is literally, "the wheel of life." That means the whole machinery of your life. The tongue not only defiles you, but it touches everything you touch. It goes beyond the body to touch every participant in the circle of your life.

The tongue's influence is a channel for the forces of hell—*"and is set on fire by hell."* It is the very center of destruction and ruin. James also describes the combative nature of the tongue. *"For every species of beasts and birds, of reptiles and creatures of the sea, is tamed and has been tamed by the human race. But no one can tame the tongue. It is a restless evil and full of deadly poison." (James 3:7-8)* It is a restless evil. It's always ready to break out. It fights against restraint. It doesn't want to be held back. And then James says it is a *"deadly poison."* It's not only like a caged animal when it breaks out, but it carries deadly venom.

David tried to control his tongue through self-determination and discovered he couldn't do it.

> *I said, "I will guard my ways that I may not sin with my tongue; I will guard my mouth as with a muzzle While the wicked are in my presence. I was mute and silent, I refrained even from good, and my sorrow grew worse. My*

heart was hot within me, while I was musing the fire burned. (Psalms 39:1-3)

David couldn't stand it—*"Then I spoke with my tongue." (v.3b)* To correct the tongue will take spiritual heart surgery. It's a tricky thing, because it is two-faced. *"With it we bless our Lord and Father, and with it we curse men, who have been made in the likeness of God; from the same mouth come both blessing and cursing. My brethren, these things ought not to be this way." (James 3:9-10)* James says man is made in the likeness of God. So how can someone bless God, but curse other men when those men are also made in the image of God?

James concludes in verses 11 and 12 that we can't. *"Does a fountain send out from the same opening both fresh and bitter water? Can a fig tree, my brethren, produce olives, or a vine produce figs? Nor can salt water produce fresh." (James 3:11-12)* James' question is rhetorical—meaning it's not really a question. It's a conclusion. One spring doesn't pour forth two kinds of water. One type of plant doesn't produce two different types of fruit. A salt spring doesn't produce fresh water. The implication is that a true Christian will not make a practice of unchristian speech; and the practice of unchristian speech is evidence that the speaker is not a Christian and is therefore in danger of hell. Now you might think, "Wait a minute, once in a while there's a little bitter water that spills out of my mouth with the fresh water."

I know that. But James is being very black and white. He's stating a truism; a fresh water fountain doesn't produce salt water. And it is a truism in your life that if you have been transformed by Christ, your speech will show it.

Reflection Questions:

1. James said earlier that when it comes to speech we all stumble. The question is—do you walk, but occasionally stumble, or do you stumble all the time, but occasionally walk? How would you judge yourself in that regard?

2. We probably have different areas of weakness in regards to our speech. Some struggle with gossip, others with hurtful, negative comments, and others with dishonesty, etc. In which area are you most vulnerable?

3. Who is someone you could enlist as an accountability partner to help you and encourage you to do better in that area?

4. What plan can you put together to grow in your speech patterns?

James 3:13a

v.13a—Who among you is wise and understanding?

This may seem like an abrupt change in topic, but a close look will show that James is following a careful outline. In 1:26-27 He identified what authentic faith looked like.

- In v.26, James said true religion is demonstrated by our speech.
- In v.27a, he said true religion is seen through our good works.
- In v.27b, James said true religion is seen when one shuns worldliness.

That paragraph forms an outline for the rest of the book. In chapter 2 James dealt with showing care and concern for those in need. In the first part of chapter 3 he dealt with the use of the tongue, and now he turns to the issue of worldliness.

He'll start be contrasting worldly wisdom with godly wisdom and will continue the theme of worldliness through the 4th chapter. James begins by contrasting godly wisdom with worldly wisdom.

First James tells us that wisdom is defined by what we do, not by what we know. *"Who among you is wise and understanding? Let him show by his good behavior his deeds in the gentleness of wisdom."* Keep the broader message of the book in mind as James begins this new section. He's dealing with worldly and godly wisdom, but his overall theme is to present various tests of an authentic faith.

How do we know if our faith is real? One way is to examine if we have shunned the world system. Worldliness seeks to invade our lives at many different points. It's this issue of wisdom that James addresses first in looking that the world's attempt to highjack our hearts.

James begins this section in an unusual way. He asks who among them is *"wise and understanding."* I say it's unusual because if one is presenting another test of an authentic faith, why ask about wisdom? I would like to submit to you that James equates being wise with being a true Christian. If you are a Christian, you'll be wise, and if you're wise, you must be a Christian.

At first we may not see the connection, because we may think of wisdom as being sage, savvy, or philosophically in tune. In other words, the wise person is the one who has contemplated the great questions of life, or the person who possesses practical knowledge about life.

But remember, James is an early book of the New Testament. He's writing to Jewish Christians. Their concept of wisdom is not Greek. He is not thinking in terms of philosophical ideas. The Jewish concept of wisdom deals with a worldview that results in a particular lifestyle. Wisdom isn't just what you think; it's how you live. James is bringing that concept into the discussion and is sharing that a true believer has a particular lifestyle. He lives in wisdom.

Think of wisdom the way we do the fruit of the spirit. Remember, Paul wrote, *"But the fruit of the Spirit is love, joy, peace, patience, kindness, goodness, faithfulness, gentleness, self-control." (Galatians 5:22-23)*

The term fruit is a singular noun. Paul is not describing different fruits, but rather one fruit with different qualities. When you are saved you receive the Holy Spirit. Ephesians, chapter one describes all the blessings that are ours through Jesus Christ. *"Blessed be the God and Father of our Lord Jesus Christ, who has blessed us with every spiritual blessing in the heavenly places in Christ." (Ephesians 1:3)*

Then Paul begins to list all those blessings. In verses 13 and 14 he tells us that one of the blessings is that when we become a Christian we receive the Holy Spirit. *"In Him, you also, after listening to the message of truth, the gospel of your salvation—having also believed, you were sealed in Him with the Holy Spirit of promise, who is given as a pledge of our inheritance, with a view to the redemption of God's own possession, to the praise of His glory." (Ephesians 1:13-14)*

All the different qualities of the fruit that characterizes the Holy Spirit, is yours. However, that fruit may be present, but not fully mature. All those characteristics describe your new life in Christ, but there is room for them to grow and develop. If you are truly saved, you'll possess the fruit of the Spirit. But that does not mean the fruit will show itself in abundance. There is room to grow, but it will be there in its beginning stages. As you learn to walk in the Spirit the different facets of His nature (fruit) will show itself as you mature in your faith.

So it is with wisdom. You may not possess wisdom in abundance, but it will be there in seed form if you are saved. So this passage serves two purposes. First it provides another test to measure the authenticity of one's profession of faith. But then also, for the true Christian, it gives a picture of the growth God desires every Christian to experience. If you're a Christian, you'll walk in wisdom, but you don't yet walk in all the wisdom you can. There is room for improvement. Therefore, this passage gives a picture of where we need to grow.

Reflection Questions:

1. The fruit of the Spirit describes motives and attitudes that are present when the Holy Spirit is in control of a life—love, joy, patience, etc. The wisdom of the Spirit (*"Godly wisdom"*) describes the actions that are present when the Holy Spirit is in control of a life. Can you think of actions that would be observable if someone were under the influence of the Holy Spirit?

2. In what ways do you evidence of the Spirit's wisdom in you?

3. In what areas do you need to grow in regard to the Spirit's wisdom?

James 3:13b

v.13b—Let him show by his good behavior his deeds in the gentleness of wisdom.

This picture of wisdom is very particular. James describes it as the *"the gentleness of wisdom."* I think he specifically uses that phrase. Even if we qualify wisdom to refer to our lifestyle, as opposed to simply one's philosophies, that realm of practical living must be narrowed even still. For example, one can be wise, or sage in how they attend to business. They not only have a particular philosophy of business, but they engage in particular practices. We would call those practices wise. But we can't use that to measure one's faith. There are many who behave wisely in different areas of life, but that behavior does not prove or disprove their profession of faith.

"Gentleness of wisdom" is referring to a very particular area of behavior. *"Gentleness"* means, "power under control", or "restraint." That could refer to restraint in many different areas of life. However, when we look at how wisdom is described in the rest of the paragraph, it's clear James is speaking about our relationships. In verse 14 he talks about *"bitter jealousy."* In verse 17 he speaks of wisdom that is *"peaceable, gentle"* and *"full of mercy."* Then in James 4:1 he asks about *"quarrels and conflicts"* going on *"among"* them. It's clear from the context James is dealing with relationships. James wants us to know there is a difference in our relationships with people once we are born again.

"Gentleness" refers to being able to get along with others by not demanding to have your own way. That's the test of an authentic faith. Jesus expressed it this way in John 13:35. *"By this all men will know that you are My disciples, if you have love for one another."* Paul expressed the same idea in Philippians 2:1-4:

> *Therefore if there is any encouragement in Christ, if there is any consolation of love, if there is any fellowship of the Spirit, if any affection and compassion, make my joy complete by being of the same mind, maintaining the same love, united in spirit, intent on one purpose. Do nothing from selfishness or empty conceit, but with humility of mind*

regard one another as more important than yourselves; do not merely look out for your own personal interests, but also for the interests of others.

James is going to contrast worldly wisdom with godly wisdom by showing how each behaves in human relationships.

Reflection Questions:

1. Gentleness has been described as power under control. The picture that is used is a person controlling a powerful horse with a small bit in the horse's mouth. The opposite of that might be the proverbial bull in a china shop. With the bull representing recklessness and the horse representing gentleness, where would you place yourself in regards to your relationships? Are you more like the bull, or like the horse?

2. What characteristics can you think of to describe "bull-like" qualities? What characteristics can you think of to describe "horse-like" qualities? Which qualities most describe you?

3. Which qualities do you need to improve on? Which ones do you need to get better control over?

4. What steps can you take to work on these?

James 3:14a

v.14—But if you have bitter jealousy and selfish ambition in your heart, do not be arrogant and so lie against the truth.

James is going to contrast worldly wisdom with godly wisdom by showing how each behaves in human relationships. He begins first with worldly wisdom. *"But if you have bitter jealousy and selfish ambition in your heart, do not be arrogant and so lie against the truth."* James had asked who was wise. He is addressing the person who says they are wise, but in reality are not. His conclusion is that they are lying about where they truly are. I don't think he means they are trying to make people think they are wise when they are not. There's something more subtle going on here.

Notice he has admonished them not to be arrogant. I don't think he meant they were boasting about their perceived wisdom. The Greek word James used for *"arrogant,"* means to look down on another. This is the person who believes they are more advanced than others. They see themselves as being at another level, beyond those around them. And they lie in the sense that in their pride, they don't think they have an issue.

But James challenges them that their wisdom is false because of two characteristics that describe their relationships with others. Notice He begins this verse with the word *"but,"* which is designed to form a contrast. The person who is truly wise is gentle in relationships, in contrast to the person who's wisdom is worldly. *"Jealousy"* and *"selfish ambition"* form a contrast to *"gentleness."* Instead of practicing a loving restraint in their relationships, this person's relationships are affected by the two driving attitudes of *"jealousy"* and *"ambition."*

Reflection Questions:

1. In what ways does jealousy hurt relationships?

2. In what ways might ambition hinder relationships?

3. Both ambition and jealousy place things and achievement above relationships. That's why James calls it *"worldly."* What are the areas of your life that have the potential to crowd out your relationships?

4. What safeguards could you put in place to help guard against that?

James 3:14b

v.14—But if you have bitter jealousy and selfish ambition in your heart, do not be arrogant and so lie against the truth.

Instead of practicing a loving restraint in their relationships, this person's relationships are affected by the two driving attitudes of jealousy and ambition. Let's look more closely at these. James doesn't just refer to it as jealousy, but rather, *"bitter jealousy."* The Greek word for this phrase is "zelos," which can be translated in various ways.

The New International Version of the Bible translates the word as *"envy."* The Young's Literal Translation uses the term, *"zeal."* The word comes from a Greek root that means "to boil, to be fervent, or to be hot." The term is neutral and can be used in a good way, or a bad way, depending on the context.

James uses the qualifier *"bitter"* to let us know he is thinking of this term in a bad way. The word *"bitter"* means, "to be sharp with someone," or "unpleasant." This is a person who is intense in a negative way in their relationships. The term is in contrast to gentleness, i.e. showing restraint in a relationship by putting others first. So this is one who doesn't put others first, but is zealous for their own way and they are sharp or unpleasant with others, if need be, in order to get their own way. They may seem pleasant, but if you press them, they will turn mean in order to get what they want. Worldly wisdom is characterized by that selfish drive. This person knows how to get their way and will do what they have to in order to get it.

Reflection Questions:

1. Do you know any people who will do whatever they have to in order to get their own way?

2. Can you recall times when you have behaved the same way?

3. Can you think of a time when our agenda is more important than a relationship?

4. What implications might that have for our goals?

James 3:14c-15

14c-15—But if you have bitter jealousy and selfish ambition in your heart, this wisdom is not that which comes down from above, but is earthly, natural, demonic.

The second characteristic of worldly wisdom is *"selfish ambition."* This is the person who wants to succeed, but not for the sake of others. Their goals are self-centered. They live out their relationships from a lust orientation. Remember, a lust orientation is when someone is self-focused. Everything is about me; what I want, when I want it, the way I want it.

James says these characteristics are in the person's heart. *"But if you have bitter jealousy and selfish ambition **in your heart**."* In other words, these are internal attitudes that are part of this person's nature. As a result, they spill over into this person's relationships. It's important to understand that, because James is contrasting two approaches to life: gentleness vs. selfish ambition and sharp zeal.

He's saying these things are in a person's heart. Keep in mind; we're not at this point focusing on specific behaviors, but rather the heart condition from which behavior springs. A person with godly wisdom doesn't just act in a gentle way, but gentleness characterizes the condition of their heart, and their actions flow out of that disposition. And likewise, a person with worldly wisdom doesn't just act in a zealous, ambitious way, but rather those things characterize their heart condition, and their actions flow out of that disposition. That's why this issue of wisdom is a way to measure the reality of one's faith. If one professes to know the Lord, but their heart is filled with bitter jealousy and selfish ambition, then their profession is a lie. And we will know the condition of their heart, by their behavior.

James then identifies the source of worldly wisdom. *"This wisdom is not that which comes down from above, but is earthly, natural, demonic."* According to James, worldly wisdom comes from three sources.

1) Worldly Wisdom Is Earthly—The word *"earthly"* literally means "on the earth." Rather than having its roots in the realms of heaven, it is limited to what can only be produced by human nature.

2) **Worldly Wisdom Is Natural**—It is a product of the human condition. It's soulish. It comes from human intellect, will and emotion. It has no spiritual origin.

3) **Worldly Wisdom Is Demonic**—This means that worldly wisdom is literally, "of the devil." That sounds diabolical, like the kind of thing we would avidly avoid. But demonic wisdom doesn't always come with cloak and dagger. Remember when Peter tried to dissuade Jesus from going to the cross. Peter was putting pressure on Jesus because he loved Jesus. But Jesus responded with a rebuke, accusing him of thinking the way man thinks, instead of thinking the way God thinks. But when Jesus rebuked him, he said, *"Get behind me Satan." (Matthew 16:23)* To think with man's interests in mind, instead of God's, is Satanic.

Reflection Questions:

1. Jesus' statement to Peter makes it sound like Satan's interests and man's interests are aligned. In what ways might that be true?

2. It sounds harsh to think of worldly wisdom as demonic, but that's what James calls it. Why do you think he might refer to it in that way?

3. What does James' statement tell us about human relationships?

4. What does Jesus' statement tell us about God's priorities?

5. What implications might that have for your life, priorities, relationships?

James 3:16-17

vs.16-17—For where jealousy and selfish ambition exist, there is disorder and every evil thing. But the wisdom from above is first pure, then peaceable, gentle, reasonable, full of mercy and good fruits, unwavering, without hypocrisy.

James continues to talk about worldly wisdom. He says it results in *"disorder."* When worldly wisdom is in operation, relationships become confused and chaotic. But worse than that, it leads to *"every evil thing."* When selfish ambition and sharp zeal is driving a relationship, it opens the door to all kinds of sin.

Finally, however, James contrasts that with godly wisdom. He begins by telling us that godly wisdom is *"from above."* This is the wisdom that comes from heaven. That means this kind of wisdom isn't natural to people. It is *"pure, then peaceable, gentle, reasonable, full of mercy and good fruits, unwavering, without hypocrisy."* You see how James describes wisdom? He doesn't describe it with a definition. Instead, he shows you what true wisdom is by how it looks in a person's life. That's because true wisdom is seen in how you live.

It is *"pure."* The Greek word means to be "unmixed, unalloyed," or "untainted by any impurity." It may point to moral purity, but in this context, it especially has the sense of being free from any jealousy or selfish ambition. It is *"peaceable."* The wise person is a peacemaker. A peacemaker does not pursue peace at any cost. They do not sacrifice truth for peace, but they do sacrifice ambition and personal agenda for peace.

Seeking peace with others is a foundational issue for a true believer:

> *For the kingdom of God is not eating and drinking, but righteousness and peace and joy in the Holy Spirit. (Romans 14:17)*
>
> *Pursue peace with all men, and the sanctification without which no one will see the Lord. (Hebrews 12:14)*

> *If possible, so far as it depends on you, be at peace with all men. (Romans 12:18)*

Godly wisdom is gentle. We have already seen that means power under control. It is also *"reasonable."* That means it is easily entreated. It's willing to listen to others and even defer to them as long as truth is not violated. It knows when to yield for the sake of peace. Godly wisdom is *"full of mercy and good fruits."* Being merciful means not only having compassion for the person who is suffering as a victim, but also showing compassion to the one who is suffering because of his own doing. By adding *"good fruits,"* James means to show that mercy demonstrates itself through kind deeds toward those who have harmed us. Godly wisdom is *"unwavering."* It's committed in its allegiance to God and relationships without flip-flopping. And finally, godly wisdom is *"without hypocrisy."* It is sincere. What you see is not a mask.

Reflection Questions:

1. That's quite a list. Which characteristics would you place in the area of your strengths?

2. Which would you place in the column that says, "Things I need to work on?"

3. If you could focus on one area to ask the Holy Spirit to strengthen in your life, which would it be?

James 3:18

v.18—And the seed whose fruit is righteousness is sown in peace by those who make peace.

I like the way the Philips Translation interprets this verse. *"And the wise are peacemakers who go on quietly sowing for a harvest of righteousness in other people and in themselves." (James 3:18 Philips Translation)* In contrast to worldly wisdom that produces *"disorder and every evil thing,"* those who walk in the wisdom from above will have the impact of peace on others. And through that, righteousness will be spread.

Godly wisdom is received through conversion. This is seen even in the Old Testament. *"The fear of the LORD is the beginning of wisdom, and the knowledge of the Holy One is understanding." (Proverbs 9:10)* That kind of wisdom, however, comes to us in seed form. (As explained in previous chapters) It grows in us through maturity. The Bible does, however, give guidelines on the development of this fruit. It doesn't grow and multiply automatically. It has to be cultivated. According to Proverbs, here is how that happens.

1. Wisdom grows through humility—*"When pride comes, then comes dishonor, But with the humble is wisdom." (Proverbs 11:2)*

2. Wisdom grows through a teachable attitude—*"He whose ear listens to the life-giving reproof will dwell among the wise." (Proverbs 15:31)* *"Listen to counsel and accept discipline, That you may be wise the rest of your days." (Proverbs 19:20)*

3. Wisdom grows through diligence—*"I love those who love me; And those who diligently seek me will find me." (Proverbs 8:17)*

4. Wisdom grows through uprightness, or integrity—*"He stores up sound wisdom for the upright; He is a shield to those who walk in integrity." (Proverbs 2:7)*

Reflection Questions:

1. If you were to pick one of those four growth points to work on, which would it be?

2. What steps would you take to begin working on it?

3. In what ways, concerning this growth point, could you ask your accountability partners to pray for you?

James 4:1a

1a—What is the source of quarrels and conflicts among you?

James is asking a question of motives. It's important to not only attend to what we do, but also to ask why we do it. God is interested in our motives. That's what today's verse gets to. However, before we dive into that, it is important to review the context of this passage. The overall theme of the letter is that James is describing the tests of an authentic faith. One of those tests is that an authentic believer shuns worldliness. At the end of chapter three and all of chapter four, James explores that idea by drawing six contrasts between worldliness and godliness.

1. Worldly Wisdom Versus Godly Wisdom—3:13-18
2. Worldly Motives Versus Godly Motives—4:1-3
3. Worldly Affections Versus Godly Affections—4:4-5
4. Worldly Self-image Versus Godly Self-image—4:6-10
5. Worldly Talk Versus Godly Talk—4:11-12
6. Worldly Planning Versus Godly Planning—4:13-17

The five contrasts in chapter four flow out of the contrast at the end of chapter three. In other words, when worldly wisdom is in operation it causes *"disorder and every evil thing"*. All the contrasts in chapter four show what that looks like. We will begin, for now, by looking at the contrast between worldly motives and godly motives. James addresses this contrast in four ways.

First, James looks at what results when worldly motives are in operation. *"What is the source of quarrels and conflicts among you?"* If fighting and quarreling is happening in the church, then worldly motives are in operation. We need to be clear about something, however. Conflicts are part of church life. Jesus addressed this knowing they would arise. (Matthew 5:23-24; 18:15-17) The Apostle Paul had such a hot dispute with Barnabas over John Mark that they split into two different teams.

> *After some days Paul said to Barnabas, "Let us return and visit the brethren in every city in which we proclaimed the word of the Lord, and see how they are." Barnabas wanted to take John, called Mark, along with them also. But Paul*

> *kept insisting that they should not take him along who had deserted them in Pamphylia and had not gone with them to the work. And there occurred such a sharp disagreement that they separated from one another, and Barnabas took Mark with him and sailed away to Cyprus. But Paul chose Silas and left, being committed by the brethren to the grace of the Lord. (Acts 15:36-40)*

At some point after that (we are not told when) the group reconciled, because Paul made it clear in other writings how important Mark was to him.

> *Aristarchus, my fellow prisoner, sends you his greetings; and also Barnabas's cousin Mark (about whom you received instructions; if he comes to you, welcome him); (Colossians 4:10)*

> *Only Luke is with me. Pick up Mark and bring him with you, for he is useful to me for service. (2 Timothy 4:11)*

There is a big difference between a conflict, which is a part of every human relationship, and the type of thing James is speaking about here. The problem James is speaking about is something altogether different. He uses two words to describe their situation: *"quarrels"* and *"conflicts."* We will look more into those two words next time.

Reflection Questions:

1. Is there anyone with whom you are currently in a quarrel or conflict?

2. What steps have you taken to try and make it right?

3. What other steps might the Lord want you to take to bring about healing and peace?

James 4:1b

v.1—What is the source of quarrels and conflicts among you? Is not the source your pleasures that wage war in your members?

1) *"Quarrels"*—The word actually means "war." It's in the present tense so it's an on going situation; more like a feud, a protracted state of hostility.

2) *"Conflicts"*—This word refers to specific outbursts of hostility, fights that erupt as a part of the on going conflict. Both words are plural, so it's a chronic condition as opposed to an isolated event. James is asking where this prolonged fighting is coming from.

If conflict arises in the church, it has to be addressed, but if the conflict turns into a feud, and if when confronted the parties involved refuse to reconcile, then it's a sign they have embraced the way of the world. And that becomes a problem. *"You adulteresses, do you not know that friendship with the world is hostility toward God? Therefore whoever wishes to be a friend of the world makes himself an enemy of God." (James 4:4)*

The kind of feuding James is talking about hurts the church's witness. The 17th century Jewish philosopher, Spinoza, wryly observed, "I have often wondered that persons who make boast of professing the Christian religion—namely love, joy, peace, temperance, and charity to all men—should quarrel with such rancorous animosity, and display daily towards one another such bitter hatred, that this, rather than the virtues which they profess, is the readiest criteria of their faith."

When the protracted war continues, the first thing we have to do is get to the root of the problem. James identified it as worldly motives—*"Is not the source your pleasures that wage war in your members?" (James 4:1)* The word *"pleasure"* identifies the motivation that's driving the conflict. It seems odd to say it is pleasure. It would make sense to say the driving motivation is selfishness—but pleasure? The reason James identifies that issue is because pleasure is the motivation behind selfishness. The Greek word he used was "hedone." We get our word hedonism from it. It means a devotion to self-indulgence—making sure self is pampered in every situation.

The opposite idea is sacrifice. This is a drive that is the opposite of sacrifice. It's the longing for total, immediate satisfaction. Notice how intense it is—*"Wage war."* Picture soldiers marching in a military campaign, aimed at securing the satisfaction of their cravings. Also, it's in the present tense, so it's ongoing and relentless. Alec Motyer wrote, "All our desires and passions are like an armed camp within us, ready at a moment's notice to declare war against anyone who stands in the way of some personal gratification on which we have set our hearts."

That raises a question about pleasures. Is it wrong to desire pleasure? Is it wrong to enjoy pleasure? That depends. When is pleasure wrong? When it violates the Word, or when it becomes an end, in and of itself. 2 Timothy 3:4 speaks of the possible imbalance when it describes men being— *"lovers of pleasure rather than lovers of God."* Pleasure is to lead us to God, not to replace Him. A sumptuous meal, a breathtaking sunset, an exotic vacation, a restful nap can all be enjoyed with a thankful heart that God has provided them for us. In praising him, the pleasure magnifies his glory.

Reflection Questions:

1. What are the particular pleasures you personally enjoy in life?

2. Can you think of times when you have allowed those pleasures to take priority over your relationship with God or others?

3. In what ways have you seen your pleasures *"waging war"* in your heart?

James 4:2a

v.2a—You lust and do not have; so you commit murder. You are envious and cannot obtain; so you fight and quarrel.

James comments that his readers, *"do not have,"* and they *"cannot obtain."* The idea is that as long as they seek satisfaction selfishly, they will never get what they want, even when they achieve the objective they think will get them their satisfaction. The drive to obtain pushes one to murder. I don't think James means that literally. He is writing the church, so it is doubtful murder was something that was practiced frequently enough that he would need to mention it in his letter to the churches.

Most likely, he is referring to relational murder. Unsatisfied lust leads people to harm relationships. We destroy reputations, tarnish another's good name, or become so angry that hatred boils up within the heart. Jesus said that was murder. (Matthew 5:21-22) James is saying at the heart of human conflict is selfishness.

If people were truly selfless, how many church splits would be averted, how many marriages saved, how many friendships restored? If there is one area where the church should be different than the world, it should be here. Conflict because truth and righteousness is opposed is one thing, but conflict because people don't get their own way, is unacceptable.

Reflection Questions:

1. In what ways would the conflicts you are presently involved in be different if you personally practiced Philippians 2:3-14?

2. If your only agenda was God's glory, in what ways would that change your position in any of the conflicts in which you may presently be involved?

3. If you are in conflict with someone, what options could you take rather than fighting or quarrelling?

James 4:2b-3

vs.2b-3—You do not have because you do not ask. You ask and do not receive, because you ask with wrong motives, so that you may spend it on your pleasures.

When worldly motives are driving a conflict the first attempt to resolve things is to independently deal with it. *"You do not have because you do not ask."* They don't take their situation to God in prayer. Ultimately, it is because they do not trust God to meet their needs. Rather than humbly depending on God, they take matters into their own hands.

God tells us to pray for our needs. But even when the worldly person does pray, it is ineffective. *"You ask and do not receive, because you ask with wrong motives, so that you may spend it on your pleasures."* They are praying either to get their own way, or at least to get God's permission. Balaam was an example of this. King Balak wanted to hire Balaam to prophesy against Israel. Balaam wanted to go meet with the king, but when he prayed initially, the answer was no. But he kept going back to prayer until God granted him permission to go.

Sometimes it seems like our prayers can follow the same track. We pray to persuade God to allow us what we want. But prayer isn't about talking God into giving us what we want. Prayer is about listening to God to understand his will in a matter, and then agreeing with him in regard to his will. *"This is the confidence which we have before Him, that, if we ask anything according to His will, He hears us. And if we know that He hears us in whatever we ask, we know that we have the requests which we have asked from Him." (1 John 5:14-15)*

Reflection Questions:

1. When you pray over a specific matter, do you typically start by asking God what you want, or do you spend time searching and listening to understand God's will?

2. Some people resist learning God's will before petitioning him. What reasons can you think of for people to be hesitant in first seeking his will on a matter?

3. If you were to make listening before asking a regular practice in your prayer life, in what practical ways would your prayer habits change?

James 4:3

v.3—You ask and do not receive, because you ask with wrong motives, so that you may spend it on your pleasures.

How should we pray and why should we pray? For many, prayer seems like a mystery. If God already knows what he is going to do, why pray? If God is sovereign and controls everything, why pray? Here are a few reasons: We pray because we are commanded to. We pray because Jesus did. We pray because God is worthy of our time and attention. We pray to align our thinking with his will. We pray because prayer is part of God's sovereign Plan.

Thomas Aquinas wrote, "Neither do we pray in order that we may alter the divine plan, but rather that we may obtain what was divinely planned to be given in answer to prayer."

Someone once compared prayer to filling a bucket. We come to God with our needs and he "fills the bucket" with water (He answers our prayers). He could fill the bucket any way he wants, by dipping it in a lake, or filling it with a hose, etc. But instead, he chooses to fill the bucket with a faucet. Let's say the lake or the hose represent direct, miraculous intervention, and the faucet represents our prayers. He could snap his fingers and make his will unfold. In other words, he could fill the bucket with the lake or the hose. But instead, he chooses to carry out his plans through the vehicle of our prayers. The "faucet" is actually part of God's sovereign plan. So prayer isn't simply God answering our requests. Instead, prayer is the means by which God chooses to get things done.

Prayer is not outside the sovereignty of God, nor does it affect the sovereignty of God, but rather prayer is part of the sovereign plan of God. He plans to accomplish project X, but he plans to accomplish it through our prayers.

The other question I asked is—How do we pray? In its simplest form, we ask, but we must ask with the right motives. Our motives when we pray must be God's glory. The Shorter Catechism says, "The chief purpose of man is to glorify God." Consumer Christianity doesn't really believe that. Consumer Christianity believes that God is the best way to experience the good life. John Piper says, "Christ does not exist in order to make much of us, we exist in order to make much of Him."

I believe the idea is seen in the opening lines of the Lord's Prayer. *"Our Father who is in heaven, hallowed be Your name. Your kingdom come. Your will be done, on earth as it is in heaven." (Matthew 6:9-10)* We need to live with that kind of an eternal, kingdom perspective, because in the end the kingdom is the only thing that matters. In the Chronicles of Narnia, C.S. Lewis gives us a glimpse of this perspective with the statement he makes at the end of the book. He concludes Peter, Edmund and Lucy's story with these words:

> "There was a real railway accident," said Aslan softly. "Your father and mother and all of you are—as you used to call it in the Shadowlands—dead. The term is over: the holidays have begun. The dream is ended: this is the morning."
>
> And as He spoke He no longer looked to them like a lion; but the things that began to happen after that were so great and beautiful that I cannot write them. And for us this is the end of all the stories, and we can most truly say that they all lived happily ever after. But for them it was only the beginning of the real story. All their life in this world and all their adventures in Narnia had only been the cover and the title page: now at last they were beginning Chapter One of the Great Story which no one on earth has read: which goes on forever: in which every chapter is better than the one before.[16]

Someday we will all leave the "shadowlands" and live in the realm that is far more real than anything we know here. Worldliness is when we are motivated by things that only matter in the shadowlands. Let's invest our lives in the next world instead of this one.

Reflection Questions:

---

[16] C. S. Lewis, *The Last Battle*, Reprint ed., New York: HarperCollins, 2008, 228.

1. Do you see prayer more as a means of receiving from God, or as a means of furthering your relationship with God?

2. If someone were to objectively examine your prayer life, how would they answer that question for you?

3. In what ways can your prayer habits change to make prayer more about nurturing relationship with God

James 4:4a

v.4a—you adulteresses

James contrasts godliness with worldliness as a mark of authentic faith. So far, we've looked at the contrast between godly wisdom and worldly wisdom, godly motives and worldly motives. Now James contrasts godly affections and worldly affections.

James is not subtle when he launches into his next point. He shocks them by accusing them of adultery. He means to jar them from their spiritual complacency. It's an idea, however, that his readers would have been familiar with, given their Jewish background. Israel was seen as a wife, because Jehovah was called her husband. *"For your husband is your Maker, whose name is the LORD of hosts; and your Redeemer is the Holy One of Israel, who is called the God of all the earth." (Isaiah 54:5)*

When Israel turned to idols it was considered adultery. *"Do not rejoice, O Israel, with exultation like the nations! For you have played the harlot, forsaking your God. You have loved harlots' earnings on every threshing floor." (Hosea 9:1)* That same concept carried over into the church. When God's people are unfaithful to the Lord, it is considered spiritual adultery, because the New Testament clearly identifies Christ as the bridegroom and the church as His bride. *"FOR THIS REASON A MAN SHALL LEAVE HIS FATHER AND MOTHER AND SHALL BE JOINED TO HIS WIFE, AND THE TWO SHALL BECOME ONE FLESH. This mystery is great; but I am speaking with reference to Christ and the church." (Ephesians 5:31-32)*

The church's practice of adultery, however, wasn't bowing at an idol's shrine. She practiced adultery by loving the world-system. And she showed that she loved the world's system by engaging in fighting and quarrelling. The previous paragraph, in James, accused the early Christians of attacking one another and fighting for their own way. Evidently they were shrugging it off as normal behavior. James' point is that that's normal behavior, if you're part of the world, but not as a part of the church. The implication is that we are the bride of Christ, and to engage in selfish conflict is to commit spiritual adultery!

Reflection Questions:

1. It may be a new idea to think of selfish conflict as spiritual adultery. Adultery involves cheating on a spouse. In what ways is engaging in selfish conflict cheating on God?

2. Jesus once said that how we treat the "least of these" is how we treat him. (Matthew 25:40-45) We show our love for God by how we love others. With that as the standard of measure, how strongly would you say you love God?

3. Keeping all that in mind, in what ways could you love God better?

James 4:4b

v.4b—Do you not know that friendship with the world...

"...do you not know that..." This is something they should know, but apparently they did not. That's because committing idolatry in the sense of worldliness can be subtle. When we think of it in terms of Jewish history, it's not subtle at all for someone to go and bow before an idol at a shrine. But it is subtle to bow down before a philosophy. And that's what it is when we are friends with the world; we're acquiescing to a certain philosophy, and that's not obvious. So the actual act of spiritual adultery isn't as distinct in this regard as it is when someone is bowing to an idol.

The Essence of Spiritual Adultery is *"friendship with the world."* *"World"* does not refer to the planet, but rather, the world-system that governs society. To cultivate the world's friendship means to conform to its principles and aims, and to desire the approval of the world. Worldliness is the acceptance of the world's presuppositions.

It's seen in the following philosophies: Humanism—man is good and within him are the answers to life. Materialism—the only thing that can truly be said to exist is matter. Relativism—there is no absolute truth. Hedonism—pleasure is the only thing that matters. Pragmatism—results justify the means. Secularism—a philosophy of life that removes religion.

Those ideas move from philosophy to life when I allow my culture to define my values: when I allow money, power, and status to cloud my definition of success: when I think a human corporation can provide security: when I seek first a respectable, lucrative career, rather than seeking first the kingdom of heaven: when I get so caught up in my own affairs that I overlook the governing providence of God in my life. It's this secular thinking—this living without reference to the One we're supposed to live for—that's truly worldly.

Reflection Questions:

1. Out of the six worldly philosophies (Humanism, materialism, relativism, hedonism, pragmatism and secularism) which one do you struggle with the most?

2. Which one do you think is most offensive to God?

3. In what practical ways can you live in opposition to these philosophies?

James 4:4c

v.4c…hostility toward God? Therefore whoever wishes to be a friend of the world makes himself an enemy of God.

Why is worldliness considered hostile action toward God? To be hostile means to attack. Adopting worldly philosophies is a frontal attack against Christ. We can get the force of it through an example from *Our Daily Bread,* a devotional booklet. Suppose that in a certain community lives a man and his wife who love each other very much. Across the street lives a man who develops a hatred for the woman's husband. One night he invades their home and kills the husband. Although the murderer is arrested, a loophole in the law allows him to escape punishment, and he is released to return to the community. Now imagine that in a few short weeks you see the widow and her husband's murderer walking down the street together. Her arm is slipped into his arm and she looks smilingly into his face. What would you say about a woman like that? You would brand her a traitor to her husband's memory and unworthy to bear his name. We must never forget that this godless world hated Jesus enough to kill Him. One who walks arm-in-arm with a system headed by our Lord's enemies and becomes friendly with them is disloyal to Jesus Christ. Only those who keep themselves *"unspotted from the world"* have a right to bear the name Christian.

"Therefore whoever wishes to be a friend of the world makes himself an enemy of God." There are two Greek words that are important in this verse. The first translates into the English phrase, *"whoever wishes."* To our ears, this word is not as strong as James would have intended. It is more than a wish. It means to choose or determine. It is an objective decision. The other phrase is, *"makes himself."* That means to take a stand. It is a decisive act. John MacArthur, in his sermon on this passage, paraphrases it this way, "Whosoever therefore deliberately chooses to be deeply affectionate for the evil system takes his stand as the enemy of God."

The person who does this makes themself God's enemy. It's important to note: this person may not consider God their enemy, but God considers them His enemy!

Reflection Questions:

1. To be called an enemy of God is severe language. We would put an atheist or Satanist in that category, but how can someone in the church be considered an enemy of God?

2. Jesus was called a friend of sinners. How is that different from being a friend of the world?

3. People often adopt worldly philosophies in a passive way. They don't intentionally choose to oppose God. Often they don't realize they have opposed God. Do you think God gives latitude here? If we realize we are aligned with the world more than God, what does God expect us to do?

4. Can you think of any ways that God may be calling you to a lifestyle change?

James 4:5a

v.5a—Or do you think that the Scripture speaks to no purpose

That statement reveals how people slip into worldly thinking in the first place. By their actions, they reveal that they think *"Scripture speaks to no purpose."* Scripture no longer holds the highest place of authority in their life. The first Psalm shows the downward progression, but it also teaches us that that would never happen if the individual had a high regard for Scripture. *"How blessed is the man who does not walk in the counsel of the wicked, nor stand in the path of sinners, nor sit in the seat of scoffers! But his delight is in the law of the LORD, and in His law he meditates day and night." (Psalm 1:1-2)*

The blessed person submits to the authority of God's word. James, however, is inferring his readers hold a low view of Scripture. To say of them that the *"Scripture speaks to no purpose"* means that it speaks in vain, that the message holds no authoritative claim on their lives. They have taken a relativistic approach to the Bible. Its interpretation is open to personal opinion.

If we are going to develop resistance to worldliness, then we must live in submission to the Scriptures. Scripture must be the supreme rule for truth. It is higher than human philosophies. I think most Christians agree with that in principle. The rub comes when the text instructs us to do something we don't want to do. It is at that moment when we see who is really in charge of our life. Do we truly submit to the Word, or only when we agree with it?

Reflection Questions:

1. What do you believe the purpose of Scripture is?

2. Are there any commands in Scripture that you are struggling to keep?

3. If so, what would need to change in order for you to live in obedience to God's Word?

4. If those changes propose a great challenge, how can your

accountability partners pray for you?

James 4:5b

v.5b—He jealously desires the Spirit which He has made to dwell in us

This is the most difficult verse in James to translate and one of the most difficult in the New Testament. I'm going to share what I believe is the correct interpretation, though I will not be dogmatic on this. The interpretation I present is held by many (if not the majority of conservative Biblical scholars) and seems to make the most sense; at least to me, anyway.

I believe James is stating a general principle. Scripture presents the idea that God is a jealous God, but of what is he jealous? He wants our total loyalty and devotion. That might seem like a strange idea to think of God as being jealous. We often think of that in a negative way. I remember in the early years of ministry working with a couple that struggled with jealousy issues. The husband was so jealous and controlling of his wife that he would record the odometer each morning when he left for work and then read it again when he got home. She had to account for every mile she drove.

That's not the kind of jealousy the Bible is talking about. There is a righteous jealousy that's expected between spouses. If a partner were cheating on their spouse, it would be normal and expected for the other one to be jealous. God is depicted as the husband of Israel, and Christ is seen as the bridegroom of the church. When we commit spiritual adultery against God, he feels betrayed. J.I. Packer describes God's jealousy in this way, "This is not the lunatic fury of a rejected or supplanted suitor, but a zeal to protect a love-relationship." God is looking for fidelity and faithfulness.

Reflection Questions:

1. Do you love what God loves and hate what God hates? (Proverbs 6:16)

2. When looking at the list of things God hates in Proverbs 6:16, how would you describe the opposite of each item?

3. What attitudes or behaviors have you engaged in the past month that would give God cause to feel jealous?

4. Some people think the idea of God being jealous makes him insecure. How would you answer that accusation?

James 4:6-8a

vs.6-8a—But He gives a greater grace. Therefore it says, "God is opposed to the proud, but gives grace to the humble." Submit therefore to God. Resist the devil and he will flee from you. Draw near to God and He will draw near to you.

Notice this paragraph begins with the word, *"but."* That connects us to the previous paragraph. That paragraph described God's desire for relationship with believers. He jealously desires the Spirit that is in us: meaning he longs to be in relationship with us, even when we stumble. That's why he "gives a greater grace." He gives us grace to call us back when we stumble. James supports this idea with a quote from Proverbs 3:34. *"Therefore it says, 'GOD IS OPPOSED TO THE PROUD, BUT GIVES GRACE TO THE HUMBLE.'" (Proverbs 3:34 quoted in James 4:6b)*

There are two classes of people described here: the proud and the humble. The proud is the independent person who strives to live their life without God. They can make it on their own. The humble is the person who lives in a state of dependence on God. That place of dependence should lead someone to place themselves under the authority and control of God. God extends grace to that person to empower them to live in obedience to him.

Therefore, James issues the following command. *"Submit therefore to God. Resist the devil and he will flee from you."* Submitting and resisting are two sides of the same coin. Submitting to God includes resisting the devil, and resisting the devil includes submitting to God. To *"resist"* means to "take your stand against" How do we do that? James answers that question in the next line. *"Draw near to God and He will draw near to you."* Drawing near is an act of the heart. You can draw near in any place or circumstance. John Piper defines it this way, "It is a directing of the heart into the presence of God who is as distant as the holy of holies in heaven, and yet as near as the door of faith." To direct the heart towards God involves submission to him. When we live in a dependency on God our minds are directed toward him, looking to understand his ways and his will. Notice also the order. First we submit to God, and then we resist the devil. Resistance against the devil is futile if we do not first submit to God.

Reflection Questions:

1. What reasons can you think of for pride receiving such a severe response from God?

2. What might be some signs of a person who is living independently from God?

3. If pride were on the one-yard line, and humility were on the 50-yard line, where would you place yourself?

4. What practical changes could you make to move down field five yards?

James 4:8b-9

vs.8b-9—Cleanse your hands, you sinners; and purify your hearts, you double-minded. Be miserable and mourn and weep; let your laughter be turned into mourning and your joy to gloom.

What does it mean to submit to God and resist the devil? We saw last time it includes drawing near to God, but James goes on and says it's done in other ways as well. *"Cleanse your hands, you sinners; and purify your hearts, you double-minded."* He calls them *"sinners"* to get their attention. They're *"double minded"* in that they're trying to live in two worlds. James' use of *"cleansing"* and *"purifying"* goes back to Jewish ceremonial practice.

> *Aaron and his sons shall wash their hands and their feet from it; when they enter the tent of meeting, they shall wash with water, so that they will not die; or when they approach the altar to minister, by offering up in smoke a fire sacrifice to the LORD. So they shall wash their hands and their feet, so that they will not die; and it shall be a perpetual statute for them, for Aaron and his descendants throughout their generations. (Exodus 30:19-21)*

The priests washed their hands in a bowl that was called a laver. It was a basin with water in which the priests had to wash from the elbow to the tip of the hand before entering the tabernacle to serve at the altar. The washing was not so much about cleansing germs, as it was a symbol of cleansing sin. The New Testament equivalent is found in Ephesians 5:26, where Paul wrote, *"...so that He might sanctify her, having cleansed her by the washing of water with the word."* We fight by regularly bathing in Scripture, because that cleanses us from the world: not the cleansing of salvation, but the cleansing of sanctification. Daily washing will keep the contamination of the world from infecting our minds and hearts.

Then James gives another piece of instruction. *"Be miserable and mourn and weep; let your laughter be turned into mourning and your joy to gloom."* This isn't saying that we are not to laugh or enjoy life, but James wants to demonstrate how seriously we need to look at our worldly ways. He's saying we need to live a repentant lifestyle, not being a condemned person, but one who is constantly aware of the need for grace and mercy. One who lives with that orientation is sensitive to the convicting work of the Holy Spirit, is teachable and keeps short accounts with God and others.

Reflection Questions:

1. Looking at the three characteristics of one who lives a repentant lifestyle (sensitivity to the convicting work of the Holy Spirit, is teachable and keeps short accounts), what would you identify as your greatest need for growth?

2. Once you have identified that area, think about the kind of person you would like to be. For example, if the growth area were sensitivity to the Holy Spirit, you might say, *I want to be the kind of person who listens closely to that inner voice and obeys its promptings*. How would you describe the kind of person you would like to be?

3. What one small step could you take to move you in that direction? For example, using the same item mentioned in #2, a small step might be to say a simple prayer each morning, *Lord help me to listen to your voice today*. It doesn't get you to the full goal, but it is a small step that establishes a habit that will be a beginning point for forming your conception of who you are. What step would you identify?

James 4:10

v.10—Humble yourselves in the presence of the Lord, and He will exalt you.

What does it mean to submit to God and resist the devil? We saw last time it includes drawing near to God, staying cleansed by the Word and living a repentant lifestyle. Then James issues another command—*"Humble yourselves in the presence of the Lord, and He will exalt you."*

To humble yourself means living in dependence on the Lord, as opposed to depending on your own strength and wisdom. That lifestyle is in total opposition to the ways of the world. In fact, it strikes against the major philosophies of worldliness.

1) Pragmatism says results are what matters, so do what works. The lie behind pragmatism is that the end justifies the means. With pragmatism we sought meaning and purpose through our own resources, but now we find true purpose and meaning through Christ. The journey is not only as important as the destination, but actually effects which destination we arrive at.

2) Relativism says there is no absolute truth. Each must discover his or her own truth. Relativism seeks justification for personal beliefs, but now, we are truly justified through Christ, standing on His eternal, absolute truth.

3) Hedonism says all that matters is pleasure, so live for that. The lie behind hedonism is that there is no eternity so the only pleasure we will have in life is what we experience now. The hedonist seeks escape from the consequences of the reality of eternity. In Christ, however, we find true pleasure in glorifying God, and won't have to shrink in shame at his appearing.

4) Humanism says there is no God. Mankind is the answer to all his or her needs. The lie behind humanism is that at the core, humans are good and need no divine help to realize their full potential. But the Bible teaches that humans are infected with the disease of sin and need a gracious God to forgive and rescue mankind from death.

All of this comes down to our self-image. Either we view ourselves as the masters of our fate (which is what the Bible would call pride), or we live with a dependence on Christ and his righteousness (which is what the Bible would call humility).

Characteristics of the proud	Characteristics of the humble
Life is about what I accomplish	Life is about Jesus Christ
Truth is what I decide	Truth is a person: Jesus Christ
What's important is that I'm happy	What's important is that God is glorified
I'm a good person and have the answers to life within myself	I'm a sinner in need of grace & mercy

Reflection Questions:

1. In what ways do you see these philosophies influencing your life?

2. Thinking about the Biblical worldview that stands opposed to each worldly philosophy, what behaviors or attitudes would you need to work on to make those philosophies more a part of your life?

3. How specifically could your accountability partners pray for you as a response to your answer in question #2?

James 4:11a

v.11a—He who speaks against a brother or judges his brother, speaks against the law and judges the law;

The phrase, *"speak against,"* means "to talk against, to defame, to slander, to speak evil of." However, the term is more than slander, or gossip, or talking behind someone's back. It literally means to speak down to someone, to speak as if you are above the other person. Though James is writing about speech, his real focus is the heart behind the speech. When we talk down to someone, we are placing ourselves first, or above him or her. Even though the immediate sin is speaking against a brother or sister, the only reason someone would do that is because self is on the throne of the heart.

Notice that *"speaking against a brother"* is *"speaking against the law."* And also, *"judging a brother"* is *"judging the law."* The *"law"* refers to the perfect, royal law, as mentioned in 1:25 and 2:8.

> *But one who looks intently at the perfect law, the law of liberty. (James 1:25)*

> *If, however, you are fulfilling the royal law according to the Scripture, "YOU SHALL LOVE YOUR NEIGHBOR AS YOURSELF," you are doing well. (James 2:8)*

We saw in previous studies that what James is talking about is the law of love, because at the heart of all the law is love. That's why the two greatest commandments are to love God and others. We're violating the law of love when we speak down to someone else, but it goes even deeper than that. I can speak against someone I hardly know and violate the law of love, but the offence is greater when I do that against someone I know. Notice how James refers to *"brother"* repeatedly in this section.

> *Do not speak against one another, **brethren**. He who speaks against a **brother** or judges his **brother**, speaks against the law and judges the law; but if you judge the law, you are not a doer of the law but a judge of it. There is only one Lawgiver and Judge, the One who is able to save and to destroy; but*

who are you who judge your neighbor? (James 4:11-12 Emphasis Added)

When we slander those in the church, we are sinning against family. To speak against a sister or brother is to break God's law and is seen as an attack against it. That's serious business, as we will see in the next study!

Reflection Questions:

1. Is there a difference between judging someone and criticizing someone? If so, what is the difference? When does it move beyond criticism to judging?

2. Often we judge ourselves by our intentions, but others by their actions. In doing that, we are inferring intentions and motives onto them. When talking about someone else, give an example of the kind of speech that infers motives or intentions.

3. In what ways would our speech change if we didn't assume motives for others?

James 4:11b-12

vs.11b-12—but if you judge the law, you are not a doer of the law but a judge of it. There is only one Lawgiver and Judge, the One who is able to save and to destroy;

To place oneself above the law is idolatry. It's committing the same sin Eve committed. *"For God knows that in the day you eat from it your eyes will be opened, and you will be like God, knowing good and evil." (Genesis 3:5)* Eve violated God's law in order to *"be like God."* She put herself in the place of God. James makes the connection with idolatry in verse 12. He says we place ourselves in the position of a judge over the law, but there's only one lawgiver, and that is God. Connecting the dots, we are putting our self in the position of God when we speak against a brother or sister. Every time we speak down to, or against someone, we are placing self in the position of God. That is because only God has the right and knowledge to judge intention and motive. At its heart, that sin is Satanic, because rebellion against God in order to exalt self is exactly what Satan did when he fell.

James then asks a tough question. *"But who are you who judge your neighbor?" (James 4:12)* It reminds me of a story I heard about two taxidermists. They had stopped before a window in which an owl was on display. They immediately began to criticize the way it was mounted. Its eyes were not natural; its wings were not in proportion with its head; its feathers were not neatly arranged; and its feet could be improved. When they had finished with their criticism, the old owl turned his head...and winked at them.

James is asking, "Who do you think you are to speak against brother or sister in the Body of Christ?" Certainly, there are differences among us (gifts, talents, personalities, abilities, education, background, etc.), and differences of opinions are to be expected, but distinction of one's value is what is in focus here. When someone speaks down to and against another, they place themselves above others. They deem themselves as having greater value than the one they are judging. People say they don't see themselves as better than others, but they demonstrate otherwise with the free sharing of their gossip, slander and judgment. We need language that doesn't divide, but unites the body of Christ.

Reflection Questions:

1. Can you identify the last time you spoke critically about someone who wasn't present to defend or explain himself or herself? (Be honest)

2. (Continuing to be brutally honest)—What was your motivation for sharing the things you said?

3. What do you think God's opinion of that would be? In light of that, how do you think you should pray?

4. What should you do if someone starts to share damaging or critical information about another person with you?

James 4:13-17

vs.13-17— Come now, you who say, "Today or tomorrow we will go to such and such a city, and spend a year there and engage in business and make a profit." Yet you do not know what your life will be like tomorrow. You are just a vapor that appears for a little while and then vanishes away. Instead, you ought to say, "If the Lord wills, we will live and also do this or that." But as it is, you boast in your arrogance; all such boasting is evil. Therefore, to one who knows the right thing to do and does not do it, to him it is sin.

James starts off by saying, *"come now, you who say..."* You can just hear the attitude of disapproval in his tone, can't you? He's going to rebuke them—not because they plan, but because of the way they plan. Notice in James' example, their plan has six components.

1. They planned when they would go—*"today or tomorrow"*
2. They planned what they would do—*"we will go"*
3. They planned where they would go—*"to such and such a city"*
4. They planned how long they would go—*"and spend a year there"*
5. They planned their purpose for going—*"and engage in business"*
6. They planned the intended result of their trip—*"and make a profit"*

The problem wasn't that their planning was wrong; it's just that it was incomplete. They planned without God. James corrects their presumption. *"Yet you do not know what your life will be like tomorrow." (James 4:14a)* We plan like we're in control of our lives. An anonymous author once said, "Write your plans in pencil, then give God the eraser." That's pretty good advice.

We plan like we are in control of our death. But James reminds us, *"You are just a vapor that appears for a little while and then vanishes away." (James 4:14b)* James wants his readers to plan, but to do so with God in the equation. *"Instead, you ought to say, 'If the Lord wills, we will live and also do this or that.'" (James 4:15)* Planning without acknowledging God is pride. *"But as it is, you boast in your arrogance; all such boasting is evil. Therefore, to one who knows the right thing to do and does not do it, to him it is sin." (James 4:16-17)*

Why is it sin to plan without God? Because that type of planning assumes that life is our right. But the harsh truth is, we have no rights. We know this, but it's easy to make plans and leave God out. When you plan, consider doing it this way:

1. Seek God's will through His Word to understand his wisdom over the matter.
2. Seek counsel from others.
3. Listen to the motives and desires of your heart, to make sure you are not reading the leading of the Lord into the situation to justify what you want to do.
4. Submit your way to the Lord and ask Him to direct your steps.
5. If your motives are clear and you're within the boundaries of Scripture, then make a decision.
6. But always hold your plans loosely, making allowance for the sovereign will of God to providentially change your course.

It's a comfort to trust in God's sovereignty, because that means it is God who governs your life—not chance, or luck, not your enemies, not disease, nor the devil. If I place my life in the hands of a sovereign God then I can face an uncertain future because I know five things.

1. I know He is Omniscient. He has all the details covered.
2. I know He is Sovereign and able to orchestrate events to bring about his desired outcome.
3. I know I'm immortal until God's work for me is done.
4. I know my accomplishments are in God's hands so ego does not have to get in the way.
5. I know He has prepared an eternal reward for those who are faithful to Him, so I do not need to fear outcomes.

Reflection Questions:

1. What plans or goals do you have set for your life right now?

2. Judging on a scale from one to ten, with one being (Not at all) and ten being (All the time), how much have you included God in the planning process?

3. What practical steps could you take to move that number one or two digits closer to a ten?

James 5:1-3

vs.1-3—Come now, you rich, weep and howl for your miseries which are coming upon you. Your riches have rotted and your garments have become moth-eaten. 3 Your gold and your silver have rusted; and their rust will be a witness against you and will consume your flesh like fire. It is in the last days that you have stored up your treasure!

James is using a rhetorical device, which is called an apostrophe, a turning away from his real audience to address some other group.

I hold to that view for three reasons: In the previous paragraph he refers to his readers as "brother," but here he is obviously addressing a different group. Secondly, his tone has changed. There is no instruction, only condemnation. Finally, this is a technique the Old Testament writers, like Isaiah and Amos, used. But why did James address people who would never read what he wrote? It would be an encouragement to the oppressed who did read his letter. He is letting them know God sees and will judge all injustices. It also stands as a warning to the church so they never become oppressive toward others.

He speaks to the unjust rich about judgment. First, he describes how they should act—*"weep and howl."* This is not a call to repentance. It's too late for that. Instead, this is a forecast of how they will react when judgment comes. Second, he describes what is coming—*"miseries which are coming upon you."* The miseries he speaks of, could refer to two things, either the destruction of Israel in 70 A.D. and again in 135 A.D., or the horrors they will experience when facing God in judgment. Either way, he is warning of destruction to come.

He issues four indictments against the rich.

A. Hoarding—*"Your riches have rotted and your garments have become moth-eaten. Your gold and your silver have rusted; and their rust will be a witness against you and will consume your flesh like fire. It is in the last days that you have stored up your treasure!"* (James 5:2-3) They have hoarded their goods for so long that moths, rust and rot have corrupted them. What's the difference between hoarding and saving?

1. Hoarding is improperly using the wealth the Lord has given us. God has given so we can give to others. Randy Alcorn said, "God prospers me not to raise my standard of living but to raise my standard of giving. God gives us more money than we need so that we can give generously."[17]

2. Hoarding speaks of a person who finds his satisfaction in things rather than God.

3. Hoarding shows no awareness of God's judgment. God calls us to be stewards of the material resources He blesses us with, and expects us to give an account for how we manage those resources. James has touched on this theme numerous times in this short letter. It was evidently a significant issue in the lives of his readers. We will look at the other indictments in the next study.

Reflection Questions:

1. From one to ten (One being a minimalist and ten being a hoarder) where would you mark yourself?

2. Do you have things stored that you have not used or looked at for two years or more? Would you consider getting rid of them?

3. If so, what has kept you from cleaning out excess things?

4. What steps could you take to begin simplifying your life?

---

[17] Randy Alcorn, *The Treasure Principle: Unlocking the Secret of Joyful Giving*, Updated Edition, Colorado Springs, CO: Multnomah, 2017.

James 5:4-6

> ***vs.4-6—Behold, the pay of the laborers who mowed your fields, and which has been withheld by you, cries out against you; and the outcry of those who did the harvesting has reached the ears of the Lord of Sabaoth. You have lived luxuriously on the earth and led a life of wanton pleasure; you have fattened your hearts in a day of slaughter. You have condemned and put to death the righteous man; he does not resist you.***

In our last study we began to list four indictments James levels against his imaginary audience of wealthy, unjust sinners. First he accused them of hoarding. Let's look at the other three.

B. Injustice—*"Behold, the pay of the laborers who mowed your fields, and which has been withheld by you, cries out against you; and the outcry of those who did the harvesting has reached the ears of the Lord of Sabaoth." (James 5:4)* In the ancient world laborers were paid at end of each day. They literally lived hand to mouth. If there was no pay, they went hungry. James says their cry reaches the ears of the *"Lord of Sabaoth."* That is a title that means, "The Lord of Hosts." He is the One who commands all of heaven. It is an Old Testament designation, occurring 23 times in Malachi alone. It is used here to speak comfort to the poor, that the sovereign God who sees all will judge the oppressive rich.

C. Indulgence—*"You have lived luxuriously on the earth and led a life of wanton pleasure; you have fattened your hearts in a day of slaughter." (James 5:5)* God is angry because wealthy employers were living in luxury while their workers were hardly able to eek out an existence. The word for *"luxuriously"* means to live a life of ease. The wealthy lived without any sense of sacrifice. They were lovers of pleasure, more than lovers of God. The Bible says that in the last days indulgence and pleasure seeking will increase. That is certainly true in America. It is the land of pleasure and entertainment. We have taken indulgence to a whole new level. The indulgence that James addressed is especially evil because the wealthy were exploiting the poor in order to live at that level.

D. Oppression—*"You have condemned and put to death the righteous man; he does not resist you." (James 5:6)* The rich man oppresses and the poor are powerless to withstand. James is painting an extreme picture. I have asked how we might respond to a message like this. Here are a few things that came to my mind. See if any of these resonate with you.

1. Serve the poor. Find ways to help those with less in our communities.
2. Treat your blessings as a stewardship. God has blessed us so that we can be a blessing to others.
3. Take no pleasure in the judgment of the wicked. God will deal with the wicked, either in this life or the next, but that should not be our focus.
4. Be patient in your own suffering when you are oppressed.
5. Remove class distinctions in the church.
6. Treat employees with fairness and dignity.
7. Don't envy the rich. Be content with what you have.

The world values money. God values justice.

Reflection Questions:

1. Of the six suggestions listed above, which do you need to work on the most?

2. What practical steps could you take to improve in that area?

3. If God could look over your budget and make some adjustments, what kinds of changes do you think he would make?

James 5:7-9

> *vs. 7-9—be patient, brethren, until the coming of the Lord. The farmer waits for the precious produce of the soil, being patient about it, until it gets the early and late rains. You too be patient; strengthen your hearts, for the coming of the Lord is near. Do not complain, brethren, against one another, so that you yourselves may not be judged; behold, the Judge is standing right at the door.*

The great New England preacher Phillips Brooks was noted for his patience. At times, however, even he struggled with impatience. One day a friend saw him feverishly pacing the floor.
"What's the trouble, Mr. Brooks?" he asked. "The trouble is that I'm in a hurry, but God isn't!" Ever been there? I sure have!

The first insight I want to look at from James is a key to developing patience. It has to do with what we truly value. We get a clue from his farming illustration. Notice the farmer is waiting over the fruit. But what is the fruit? It's described as *"precious produce."* A sub-theme throughout the letter has been that God is working in us through trials to produce maturity. (James 1:2-4) That's the precious produce—conformity to the image of Christ. Like the farmer that waits over the fruit, we must set our hearts on maturity and Christlikeness.

We can be patient when the world assaults us because we have set our hearts on becoming "mature and complete," and our trial is the only means by which that will happen. So we have to have the right values if we are going to be patient.

Notice something else about the verse. The farmer waits for the produce, but he waits *"until"* the early and late rains. The *"early rains"* came in late October and produced germination and seed growth. The *"later rains"* came in April and May and promoted growth to maturity. James ties this to the coming of the Lord.

Notice the parallel:

- *Be patient, brethren, until the coming of the Lord.*
- *The farmer waits…until it gets the early and late rains.*

The farmer is motivated by his hope that the rains will come. In the same way, we are to be motivated by our hope that Christ is returning. One of the temptations when we are waiting, is to complain. James addresses that as well. *"Do not complain, brethren, against one another, so that you yourselves may not be judged; behold, the Judge is standing right at the door." (James 5:9)*

A guide at Blarney Castle in Ireland was explaining to some visitors that his job was not always as pleasant as it seemed. He told them about a group of disgruntled tourists he had taken to the castle earlier in the week. "These people were complaining about everything. They didn't like the weather, the food, their hotel accommodations, the prices, everything. Then to top it off, when we arrived at the castle, we found that the area around the Blarney Stone was roped off. Workmen were making some kind of repairs. The woman who had complained the most said, 'This is the last straw! I've come all this way, and now I can't even kiss the Blarney Stone.' 'Well, you know,' answered the guide, 'according to legend, if you kiss someone who has kissed the stone, it's the same as kissing the stone itself.' The woman retorted, 'And I suppose you've kissed the stone.' The guide answered, 'Better than that. I've sat on it.'"

Often in our impatience we find ourselves complaining. It is interesting that of all the ways James could have applied his teaching about patience, he raised this one application about complaining. Why does James mention this? I think because it is the one thing we are often freest to express. It would be easy to disregard complaining, but notice, it's not just the first item on James' list, but it's the only item on his list. I think that's because complaining is the first indicator that we are impatient. It reveals that our focus is off of the fruit God is working to grow in us, and that our expectations are focused on something other than the return of Christ.

Reflection Questions:

1. The second coming of Jesus was a message of hope for James' readers because they were suffering persecution. It was a message that brought comfort. Do you think that message has changed in our day?

2. In a prosperous and free society the message of the second coming of Jesus tends to focus more on curiosity than hope. What might be the reasons for that?

3. In what ways could we use the message of Christ's return to introduce hope to the hurting?

James 5:10-11

vs.10-11—As an example, brethren, of suffering and patience, take the prophets who spoke in the name of the Lord. We count those blessed who endured. You have heard of the endurance of Job and have seen the outcome of the Lord's dealings, that the Lord is full of compassion and is merciful.

James tells us to take a look at some good examples. First he talks about the prophets in general. Many Old Testament prophets went through great suffering. Consider Jeremiah: he was the object of an intense manhunt. His writings were destroyed. He was thrown into a cistern and left in the mud to die. In spite of all that, he stayed obedient and continued to preach. He could have stopped his suffering. He would have simply had to stop preaching. But he didn't. He continued to declare the word of the Lord, in spite of the personal suffering it brought him.

Then James mentions Job. James' readers would have been familiar with Job's story. Maybe you're not. Catastrophe destroyed his farm buildings and his livestock. He was left penniless. Then in a freak accident all his children were killed. On top of that he was afflicted with a disease that covered his body from head to toe with painful boils. Everything went wrong; even his wife kicked him when he was down. She told him to curse God and die! Job was a mess. Emotionally he regurgitated all over the place. His book is filled with pain and struggle. He couldn't understand why God was allowing those things to happen to him. He had some hard questions about life. We see his human frailty. Yet the Bible says in all that, Job did not sin. I'm glad the Bible records both his struggle and his victory, because that way we can relate. He had a hard time accepting what was happening to him, but in spite of it all, Job remained faithful.

James is saying that patience means five things: 1) Patience means remaining obedient, even when that obedience causes you to suffer. 2) Patience means remaining faithfully committed to God, even though you don't understand why he's allowing bad things to happen. 3) Patience means not complaining against others when you're going though a difficult time. 4) Patience means keeping your focus on the prize, which is conformity to the image of Christ. 5) Patience means keeping your hope fixed on the soon return of Jesus Christ. If we do that, then we can withstand the onslaught of the world system.

Reflection Questions:

1. What are the situations that most try your patience?

2. The heart of patience is trust. A person who can trust God's sovereignty is better able to face life circumstances with a reliance on God and his ability to orchestrate that which he chooses. Keeping that in mind, look back at the areas you identified as triggers for impatience and try to identify any lack of trust that stands at the root of your impatience.

3. Instead of focusing on being more patient, what steps could you take to build more trust in the areas you identified?

James 5:12a

v.12—But above all, my brethren, do not swear, either by heaven or by earth or with any other oath; but your yes is to be yes, and your no, no, so that you may not fall under judgment.

Another sign of an authentic faith is that we speak the truth. Actually James says this sign is the most prominent of all. Notice he begins the verse with—*"But above all."* I think the reason James lists this as such a priority is because honesty is at the core of one's relationship with God. Our salvation is founded on truth. Let me state that by coming from a different direction. Our enemy (Satan) is called *"the father of lies." (John 8:44)* That's because deception is at the heart of his nature. In the same way, truth is at the heart of God's nature. That's why the Bible says it is impossible for God to lie (Hebrews 6:18), because there is no deception in him. Lies are told to protect or to get one's way. But God is sovereign and completely perfect, so he has no need for protection and as sovereign of all creation he does not need to manipulate to get his way. Thus, there is no need for him to lie. God doesn't tell the truth; He is truth. If you are born again you are given a new heart. And that heart reflects the nature of the God who lives in you. Thus, honesty will be at the heart of who you are.

James begins his admonition by saying, *"do not swear."* He's talking about oaths. An oath means framing your words so that they are binding, which implies that when an oath is not used, the words may not be true. The real issue isn't whether or not we should take an oath. There are times when oaths are appropriate: such as wedding vows, or testifying in court. The real issue is whether or not we are truthful. We don't tell the truth because we've taken an oath; we tell the truth because we're truthful. What, therefore, is James' caution against oaths about? Helmut Thielicke, a German scholar helps us see why James had a problem with making oaths:

> Whenever I utter the formula "I swear by God," I am really saying, "Now I'm going to mark off an area of absolute truth and put walls around it to cut it off from the muddy floods of untruthfulness and irresponsibility that ordinarily overruns my speech." In fact, I am saying even more than this. I am saying that people are expecting me to lie from the start. And just

because they are counting on my lying I have to bring up the big guns of oaths and words of honor.[18]

What he's saying is that Oaths compartmentalize the truth. They say, "God is invited into this part of my life, but not others." But life can't be divided into compartments. An oath as James is describing implies that when I don't make an oath I'm free to lie. But the proper purpose of an oath is not to force me to tell the truth. An oath is designed to officially declare a covenant binding.

James brings this up because the Jews abused oaths. They had elaborate rules, that if you swore by the temple, you weren't bound by your oath, but if you swore by the gold of the temple, you were bound. It was like saying, "I had my fingers crossed, so I really didn't mean what I said." Jesus addressed this very thing in Matthew 23:16-22

> Woe to you, blind guides, who say, "Whoever swears by the temple, that is nothing; but whoever swears by the gold of the temple is obligated." You fools and blind men! Which is more important, the gold or the temple that sanctified the gold? And, "Whoever swears by the altar, that is nothing, but whoever swears by the offering on it, he is obligated." You blind men, which is more important, the offering, or the altar that sanctifies the offering? Therefore, whoever swears by the altar, swears both by the altar and by everything on it. And whoever swears by the temple, swears both by the temple and by Him who dwells within it. And whoever swears by heaven, swears both by the throne of God and by Him who sits upon it.

Reflection Questions:

1. Have you ever reinforced something you said by stating, "I swear to you…?"

2. What was the reason you felt the oath was necessary?

3. Can you think of any behaviors or speech patterns in your life that could lead to people doubting your word without an oath?

---

[18] Andrew Gioulis quoting Helmut Thielicke, Grace Quotes, n.c., Accessed March 2019, http://gracequotes.org/quote/whenever-i-utter-the-formula-i-swear-by-god-i-am/.

4. What things do you need to work on so that when you say yes or no, it is enough?

James 5:12b

v.12—But above all, my brethren, do not swear, either by heaven or by earth or with any other oath; but your yes is to be yes, and your no, no, so that you may not fall under judgment.

James and Jesus teach that we are to tell the truth in all we say. But our culture, like the Jews, makes a lot of room for lies. Here's an example from the publication *Bits & Pieces* of some of the lies we tell

(1) The half-lie: You tell the truth, but not all the truth. Abraham did this when he claimed that Sarah was his sister. That was technically true. She was his half sister, but she was also his wife. That was the issue. He was afraid that if Pharaoh found out Sarah was his wife, that Pharaoh's guards would kill him in order to seize her for his harem.

(2) The "white" lie: These are the "innocent" lies that "don't hurt anyone." For example, you call in sick to work when you're really well.

(3) The Elastic Lie: Exaggeration, stretching the truth to make yourself look better or to evoke sympathy for your cause. Pastors are notorious for this. They often speak "evangelastically."

(4) The silent lie: The other person assumes something that is clearly false, but you don't speak up to correct it. You didn't state the lie, but you allowed them to believe the lie when you knew they were believing a falsehood.

(5) The cover-up lie: You hide your own wrongdoing with the rationalization that it would hurt the other person too much to find out the real truth.

(6) The evasive lie: you change the subject or conveniently dodge the truth by not answering directly.

(7) The technical lie: This is when you state the truth, but in such a way as to deceive. I once heard Dr. Keith Drury share in a sermon that he once had someone look at all the books in his library and ask him, "Did you read all these?" He answered, "Some of them twice." The effect was that

he had read all of them (which wasn't true) and even read some more than once (which was true).

The standard operating procedure should be to let your yes be yes. As believers in Christ, that's how we are to live.

> *If indeed you have heard Him and have been taught in Him, just as truth is in Jesus, that, in reference to your former manner of life, you lay aside the old self, which is being corrupted in accordance with the lusts of deceit, and that you be renewed in the spirit of your mind, and put on the new self, which in the likeness of God has been created in righteousness and holiness of the truth. Therefore, laying aside falsehood, SPEAK TRUTH EACH ONE of you WITH HIS NEIGHBOR, for we are members of one another. (Ephesians 4:21-25)*

Reflection Questions:

1. Looking over the list of lies above, identify the ones in which you tend to participate.

2. What motives can you identify for telling those kinds of lies? Dig deep on this one. If you answer that you did it because of fear, for example, ask yourself why? Why were you afraid? Keep asking why until you get to the root that drove the lie.

3. What actions can you take to deal with that root(s)?

James 5:13-14a

vs.13-14a—Is anyone among you suffering? Then he must pray. Is anyone cheerful? He is to sing praises. Is anyone among you sick? Then he must call for the elders

"Is anyone among you suffering?"—The word for *"suffering"* is in the present tense. This is not referring to a single episode. It's not talking about simply having a bad day. Rather, this is continual suffering. The word is also general—suffering in a variety of ways. In the beginning of the letter James said to consider it all joy when we suffer. Now he is telling his readers to pray when they suffer. We are to rejoice in what God can do with the suffering, but it is also fine to pray and ask for healing, with the caveat that our lives are surrendered to God's will. (Luke 22:42)

"Is anyone cheerful? He is to sing praises." Singing is a form of prayer, the language of the soul. I was mentoring a man once who was in a stuck place. He would pray and it seemed like he hit a wall. I suggested he take a walk on his property (he owned many acres) and go where no one would hear him and sing songs of praise to the top of his voice. He followed my suggestion and went out to his fields and sang for over an hour. Something transpired in that moment. He had a breakthrough.

"Is anyone among you sick? Then he must call for the elders of the church." The word *"sick"* means that you are incapacitated, brought low with sickness. However, the word is also very broad. It includes any serious physical, mental, emotional, spiritual, or relational problem that has become too heavy to bear. In such a case, James says to call for the elders of the church. Two questions need to be raised. Who are the elders? And, why call for the elders? The elders are the spiritual leaders in the fellowship. They are to be called because they represent the church. The entire church can't come visit you in the hospital! Also, the elders are to be preeminently people of prayer.

Notice in this situation that James places the responsibility for calling this prayer meeting on the shoulders of the one who is sick. They are expected to initiate the contact. But then the elders are to respond by going to the sick person. The reason for that is assumed by the text that the sick person is too ill to leave their bed and he or she is too weak to pray. The text also

uses the plural—*"elders."* This is important for a number of reasons. There is strength in numbers.
Also, their presence encourages the sick person with the message that "The church has not forgotten you."

Reflection Questions:

1. Short of a pastor or chaplain praying for someone in a hospital bed, we do not often see this practiced in the modern church? For what reasons do you think that might be?

2. Would you think to ask for elders to come pray for you? Why or why not?

3. Is this an antiquated practice, or do you think there is value in it? What are the reasons for your answer?

James 5:14b-15a

vs.14b-15a—anointing him with oil in the name of the Lord; and the prayer offered in faith will restore the one who is sick, and the Lord will raise him up

James says the elders are to do three specific things: 1) pray over the sick person, 2) anoint him or her with oil, and 3) pray in the name of the Lord. To *"pray over"* a person is not another way of saying they are to pray concerning a person. It literally means to pray over them, implying the person is seriously ill and unable to get up. Anointing someone with oil is not a magic talisman. There is no supernatural power in a few drops. It doesn't matter if it is oil-olive, peanut oil, or any other kind. Oil was used for medicinal purposes in that day, so some believe James is instructing them in that regard, to message it in. But oil had many more uses than that, and medicinal use was not the primary purpose.

I think James instructed the elders to use oil for three reasons. First, the oil would be a simple aid to faith. The actions reinforce the words. Second, oil is a reminder that all healing must come from God. Oil was a symbol of the Holy Spirit so applying it acknowledges that the one offering the prayer does not do the healing. It is God alone who heals. The oil became an issue of ownership and submission. Kings and priests were anointed with oil as a symbolic way to present them as people set aside for God's use. When someone is anointed with oil, they are acknowledging that they belong to God. They are set-aside for his purposes. This person is submitted to the Lord's will, whether that will is to heal them on this side of heaven, or to release the healing in eternity.

Praying *"in the name of the Lord"* is not a mantra, tag, or formula. To pray in Jesus' name implies that we are sensitive to his will and purposes. To pray in his name is to pray what he would pray if he were the one praying. We are coming before God and saying that we are representing Jesus and his will. That places a great responsibility on us to seek the will of God in prayer.

"And the prayer offered in faith will restore the one who is sick, and the Lord will raise him up." James states without qualification that the sick person will be healed. That's problematic because it is an undeniable fact

that not everyone we pray for and not everyone we anoint, is healed. Ray Pritchard helps out with this in one of his sermons:

> Most of us think of healing as "getting rid of the disease." It's like running the clock of life backwards and restoring the person to their previous state. But healing in the Bible is a very broad concept that involves coming into a right relationship with God first and foremost. Then it touches every part of life-body, soul, and spirit. It involves the healing of all broken relationships and brings us to a place where we can receive God's blessings in a new and powerful way. Healing in the Bible is not becoming what we were but becoming all that God intends us to be. When we pray for healing, we dare not focus on the physical to the exclusion of the spiritual, emotional, and relational sides of life. We are not healed until we are made whole on every level of our existence.

The complete healing that Pritchard is speaking of ultimately will happen at glorification. The most important part of the healing event is reconciliation with God. James concludes the idea by writing, *"and if he has committed sins, they will be forgiven him."* Jesus often brought the two ideas together. For example, when he healed the man who was lowered through the roof, he told the man his sins were forgiven. That to Jesus was the most important part. In fact he said in order to prove he had the authority to forgive the man's sins he would physically heal him. The physical healing was only to underscore the more important part. After all, the man would eventually get sick again and die (as we all will), but his existence after death is eternal. That is the more important part. (Luke 5:17-39)

Reflection Questions:

1. Have you ever had someone anoint you with oil and pray for your healing? What happened?

2. Do you see this practice as essential, or an optional touch? Why or why not?

3. In what ways could a church incorporate these practices into its ministry?

James 5:15b-16a

vs.15b-16a—and if he has committed sins, they will be forgiven him. Therefore, confess your sins to one another, and pray for one another so that you may be healed.

The last phrase of verse fifteen is controversial. How can praying for someone who is physically ill lead to forgiveness of sin? The idea is that God isn't just interested in one dimension of our life. He desires that we be whole: physically, spiritually, emotionally, etc. However, that doesn't mean that forgiveness of sins comes automatically with prayer for healing. The assumption is that when someone asks for healing, they're also ready to ensure that everything between them and God is settled. But also, everything between then and others is settled. James doesn't just leave us with that assumption; however, he connects the dots with verse 16. *"Therefore, confess your sins to one another, and pray for one another so that you may be healed."*

Notice, James does not say to confess so you may be forgiven, but to confess so that you may be healed. And also, he doesn't say to confess to God so that you may be healed, but to confess to one another so that you may be healed. Praying for each other, and being accountable to each other keeps us spiritually healthy and is a powerful prerequisite for physical healing. It's not an accident that *Alcoholics Anonymous* requires those going through the twelve steps to confess their sins to those whom they have wronged. There is something about clearing the air that opens the door to healing.

Reflection Questions:

1. Who are some people in your life that you would be comfortable enough to be accountable to them?

2. What would be the benefits of having an accountability partner?

3. What reasons would keep one from establishing a regular accountability meeting where they could be open and honest with another?

James 5:16b-18

vs.16b-18—The effective prayer of a righteous man can accomplish much. Elijah was a man with a nature like ours, and he prayed earnestly that it would not rain, and it did not rain on the earth for three years and six months. Then he prayed again, and the sky poured rain and the earth produced its fruit.

James moves beyond the issue of sickness and sums up his whole argument, which he began in verse 13 with a general principle of prayer. This statement applies to all prayer, not just prayer for healing. I say that because the example James uses from the life of Elijah has nothing to do with sickness. James is actually wrapping up his whole teaching on prayer in these next couple of lines. He offers a great principle as a word of encouragement—*"The effective prayer of a righteous man can accomplish much."*

It's the *"effective"* prayer that will *"accomplish much."* It's the same Greek word from which we get the term energy. It means to work. Some Bibles even translate the phrase as *"the fervent prayer..."* This kind of praying has to do with passion and sincerity. That's important, not only because of what it does say, but also because of what it does not say.

James does not refer here, to the eloquent prayer. In other words, effective praying is not dependent on the specific words you use. God is not looking for verbal formulas, or beautiful sentences. He's looking for heart. Not that we're loud and boisterous before God, but rather that we are totally invested in what we are saying. We are not asking flippantly, or casually. We're completely there.

Then to wrap everything up, James uses Elijah as an example for us to encourage us in our praying. *"Elijah was a man with a nature like ours, and he prayed earnestly that it would not rain, and it did not rain on the earth for three years and six months. Then he prayed again, and the sky poured rain and the earth produced its fruit."* (James 5:17-18)

At first we might wonder why James would use Elijah. He's one of the heroes of the faith. How can we relate to him? He prayed for God to send down fire on an altar and God responded by consuming the sacrifice with a bolt of fire from heaven. (1 Kings 18:16-45) He escaped death and was taken to heaven in a fiery chariot. (2 Kings 2) How can we relate to someone like that? But that's James' point. Yes God did amazing things through Elijah and answered his prayers, however, there's something about Elijah we need to know. He had a nature just like us. He wasn't some superhero. He was a normal human being. On one occasion he was so discouraged he begged God to let him die.

> *And he was afraid and arose and ran for his life and came to Beersheba, which belongs to Judah, and left his servant there. But he himself went a day's journey into the wilderness, and came and sat down under a juniper tree; and he requested for himself that he might die, and said, "It is enough; now, O LORD, take my life, for I am not better than my fathers." (1 Kings 19:3-4)*

He wasn't perfect, but he loved God and prayed passionately, believing in God. He had his ups and downs, but the one thing he did—he prayed. E.M. Bounds said it beautifully:

> [People] are God's method. The church is looking for better methods; God is looking for better [people.] What the church needs today is not more machinery, not new organizations, or more and novel methods, but [people] whom the Holy Spirit can use – [people] of prayer, [people] mighty in prayer. The Holy Spirit does not flow through methods, but through [people.] He does not come on machinery, but on [people.] He does not anoint plans, but [people] – [people] of prayer"[19]

If you will pray with the right motives, God will answer. In fact, because God is so faithful to answer us, prayer is a stewardship. We must not take it lightly but pray with care and fervency, for prayer sets eternal forces in motion.

Reflection Questions:

1. Can you recall an experience where you had a clear, undeniable answer to prayer? What happened?

---

[19] E. M. Bounds, *Power Through Prayer*, Norcross, GA: Trinity Press, 2011.

2. People don't often "wrestle" with God in prayer. We tend to offer up a quick word and then are done. We breathe a request while on the way to do something else, instead of taking the time to step aside from our schedule and truly wait on God. If you find that is true in your life, what reasons do you think lie at the heart of that reality?

3. What steps could be taken to change that?

James 5:19-20a

vs.19-20—My brethren, if any among you strays from the truth and one turns him back, let him know that he who turns a sinner from the error of his way will save his soul from death and will cover a multitude of sins.

James has listed several marks of an authentic faith. His final characteristic is that a true believer cares about the spiritual condition of other believers. Wandering from the faith is a danger of which we need to be aware. The New Testament speaks about it on several occasions.

> *"Keeping faith and a good conscience, which some have rejected and suffered shipwreck in regard to their faith." (1 Timothy 1:19)*

> *"But the Spirit explicitly says that in later times some will fall away from the faith, paying attention to deceitful spirits and doctrines of demons." (1 Timothy 4:1)*

> *"Take care, brethren, that there not be in any one of you an evil, unbelieving heart that falls away from the living God." (Hebrews 3:12)*

This a difficult topic because people interpret these verses according to their own theological bent. Let me show you what I mean. Some would say James is speaking about a Christian who falls away from the faith and rejects their salvation. However, before they are totally lost, a caring brother rescues them. Others would say James is speaking about someone who is in the church, but isn't really saved. They attend church, but are on their way to hell. However, a caring brother or sister helps them see the error of their way and they get saved and thus are rescued from eternal destruction. Still others would say that James is speaking of a true believer who wanders away from the faith, but they don't lose their salvation. They go on a road of destruction, but that's limited to this life. Their life will be riddled with catastrophe, but a loving brother or sister shows them the error of their ways and they are led back to the right path.

So it's either…

- A Christian who loses salvation and is potentially lost.
- A false convert who sees the light and gets truly saved.
- A Christian who falls away and is severely disciplined by God, but doesn't lose salvation.

Some argue he's a true Christian because he is identified as one of the "*brethren.*" Some say he loses salvation because it says his "*soul*" is destroyed. Others say he can't be a Christian, because other Scriptures indicate Christians can't lose their salvation. You could go around-and-around on this. The reason is because on this issue of eternal security vs. conditional security, the Bible is not black and white. Scholars can Biblically argue both sides of the issue—and they have for hundreds of years. My sense of things is that where the Bible is clearly black and white on an issue, we must be black and white on an issue, but where the Bible is ambiguous—we don't need to feel compelled to be black and white.

So what do we do with a passage like this? Do we push our personal perspective and force debate? Do we skip the passage and pretend it's not there? No. There are general principles that arise out of this passage that we can all learn from, and that's where we need to focus. Which is what we will look at in the next chapter.

Reflection Questions:

1. Have you ever had any Christian friends who have wandered away from the faith? If so, were you free to talk with them about that? If so, what were some of the reasons they offered for their present state?

2. In what ways could you talk with someone who has walked away from the faith without sounding judgmental, yet also without compromising your own faith?

3. What is it that people need most when we engage them in those kinds of conversations?

James 5:19-20b

vs.19-20—My brethren, if any among you strays from the truth and one turns him back, let him know that he who turns a sinner from the error of his way will save his soul from death and will cover a multitude of sins.

What do we do when a sister or brother stumbles? I have four observations that I believe are important for us to consider.

1. There is a danger that Christians can wander from the faith.

Let's put aside whether that means loss of salvation or not—either way—wandering is not good. And it's a danger we must be wary of. *"But the Spirit explicitly says that in later times some will fall away from the faith, paying attention to deceitful spirits and doctrines of demons." (1Timothy 4:1)* Notice here that the point of departure from the faith is doctrine. That is an important clue as to what is key in staying on track in our own faith journey.

I read a book by Jon Krakaur about Christopher Johnson McCandless. He died in 1992 at only 24 years old. He died in Alaska near Denali National Park. Chris called himself Alexander Supertramp. He left home and hid from his family, hiking around the country for two years. Finally, he moved to Alaska where he attempted to live off the land. He bought a book on edible foods in Alaska, but misidentified some potato roots. They were poisonous and blocked his system from receiving needed nutrients. Hunters found his body in his sleeping bag. He had been dead for two weeks, weighing only 65 lbs.[20]

That's how it is with false doctrine. We ingest false ideas—*"doctrines of demons"*—and it poisons us. It causes malnourishment, even though we may be exposed to church, we starve spiritually: we can attend worship: we can sing: we can pray, but our souls will not be nourished because we have been poisoned by false doctrine. Thus surrounded by food, we will starve to death.

---

[20] Jon Krakaur, *Into The Wild,* New York: Anchor Books, 1997.

2. Sin is destructive and must be avoided at all costs.

Dr. George Sweeting recollected a trip he took to Niagara Falls. He said it was spring. Ice was rushing down the river. He saw several large blocks of ice flowing toward the falls. Carcasses of dead fish were embedded in the ice and gulls by the score were riding down the river, feeding on the fish. He said:

> I watched one gull, which seemed to delay and wondered when it would leave. It was engrossed in the carcass of a fish, and when it finally came to the brink of the falls, out went its powerful wings. The bird flapped and flapped and even lifted the ice out of the water, and I thought it would escape. But it had delayed too long so that its claws had frozen into the ice. The weight of the ice was too great, and the gull plunged into the abyss.[21]

No matter how little we dabble in it, sin unchecked will lead to destruction.

Reflection Questions:

1. No one intends to get "stuck" in the ice. How does it happen that people get trapped in sin?

2. What dangers do you see in your own life that you need to be careful about?

3. If someone approached you about concern for your soul, how would you respond to him or her?

---

[21] Byron D. Klaus, "Power for Ministry: Strange Fire or Refiner's Fire", Enrichment Journal, n.d., Accessed March 2019, http://enrichmentjournal.ag.org/200003/082_powerforministry.cfm.

James 5:19-20c

vs.19-20—My brethren, if any among you strays from the truth and one turns him back, let him know that he who turns a sinner from the error of his way will save his soul from death and will cover a multitude of sins.

In the last lesson I made some observations about these verses.

1. There is a danger that Christians can wander from the faith.
2. Sin is destructive and must be avoided at all costs.

Here are two more:

3. God's grace totally restores the one who repents.

Jesus told the story about the son who asked his father for his share of the family inheritance. He took the money, left home and spent it on riotous living. When the money was gone and he was wallowing in a pig's trough, he came to his senses and realized he had made a huge mistake. He couldn't just go back home and ask to be in his father's good graces again. He decided to go back home and see if his father would take him back as a slave. But Jesus said that when the son approached the family farm, the father saw him coming form a distance and ran to him, to accept him back into the family. The point was that God's arms are open to prodigals. The young man didn't deserve the Father's warm reception. In fact, at first he had a difficult time receiving the father's forgiveness.

That's how grace is. It's hard to receive—precisely because we don't deserve it. Jesus brought the older son into the story to voice the objections we often raise.

- It's not fair.
- He's taking advantage of the father's mercy.
- He'll not learn his lesson.
- He doesn't deserve to have a party.

The father reminded both sons; it's not about keeping records. It's about resurrection. The wayward son was dead, but now he is alive—that's what matters.

4. God is pleased when we help an erring brother or sister.

James encourages us to do just that, but we need to be careful how we do that. There are three things to remember when *"turning a [sister of brother] back from the error of their ways."*

1. Check your motives—*"Brethren, even if anyone is caught in any trespass, you who are spiritual, restore such a one in a spirit of gentleness; each one looking to yourself, so that you too will not be tempted. Bear one another's burdens, and thereby fulfill the law of Christ." (Galatians 6:1-2)*

The motive is to *"restore,"* not to condemn or judge. Notice, this is also a person who is *"caught."* That means there is no doubt they are guilty. I think that speaks to making sure we get our facts straight, and don't assume guilt based on rumors. Also, Paul said we are to proceed with *"gentleness."* Don't accuse, but ask questions. Show tenderness, not anger. If we are trying to help someone, our goal is reconciliation, not punishment or exposure.

2. Clear any logs from your own eyes first—*"Why do you look at the speck that is in your brother's eye, but do not notice the log that is in your own eye? Or how can you say to your brother, 'Let me take the speck out of your eye,' and behold, the log is in your own eye? You hypocrite, first take the log out of your own eye, and then you will see clearly to take the speck out of your brother's eye." (Matthew 7:3-5)*

3. Confront in private—*"If your brother sins, go and show him his fault in private; if he listens to you, you have won your brother." Matthew 18:15*

James ends his letter abruptly. Unlike the Apostle Paul who spent an entire chapter in Romans saying goodbye—he greeted over 30 people—James just lists the final character of a true faith and then stops. No warning. We can see the end is coming because we can look on the page, but his original audience would have listened to an audible reading of the letter. So they had no idea he was at the end. He just quit. So in keeping with

James's style, I'm going to end this Bible series the way James ended his letter.

Reflection Questions:

1. If you had to talk with someone who was on a destructive path, what are some different ways you might approach the conversation?

2. What are some things you should not do or say?

3. What are some things you should make sure you do say?

Made in the USA
San Bernardino, CA
06 June 2019